Beyond the Thistle Patch

Cover design by Kent Grey-Hesselbein,

KGB Design Studio

Manchester, TN, USA

http://kghdesign.nvaazion.com/

If you like this book, you may enjoy the following titles also by Stanley J. "Stan" St. Clair:

Conspiracy in the Town that Time Forgot

ISBN 978-0-9801704-9-8 (The true story of the contract on the life of Sheriff Ron Cunningham and the FBI sting that helped take down an ex-governor – regional best seller)

Quinn

ISBN 978-0-9801704-7-4 (Novella based on the true story of how a mentally challenged boy changed the destiny of an entire family)

A Place in Time

ISBN 978-0-9801704-8-1 (A historic novella about the American Reconstruction Era, shutting down the KKK and the healing of the nation)

Reflections on Life

ISBN 978-0-9801704-1-2 (A collection of the nostalgic poetry of Stan St. Clair written over a 30-year period)

A Proud Heritage, the James Ansel Vinson Family Story

(The history and adventures of the Vinson family and their genealogy)

Beyond the

Thistle Patch

by

Stanley J. St. Clair

Edited by Rhonda St. Clair

Based on the true story

of my youth-

A tale for children of any age

© 2010 by Stanley J. St. Clair

St. Clair Publications

ISBN 978-1-935786-03-0

Printed in the United States of America by

St. Clair Publications

P. O. Box 726

Mc Minnville, TN 37111-0726

http://stclairpublications.com

Contents

𝒫𝒾𝒸𝓉𝓊𝓇𝑒𝓈

Dedication

This Book is dedicated to the memory of the following individuals who had a special impact on my life during the course of the ten year period covered herein, who have since passed from this life.

FAMILY

Ethel Melissa Runion Vinson 6-20-1891 - 9-13-1997[1]

James Ansel Vinson   1-7-1884 - 6-20-1983[1]

Marvin Woodrow St. Clair   3-15-1919 – 10-6-1980[1]

Trula Genevieve Vinson St. Clair 8-6-1909 – 4-12-2000[1]

Jesse Salem Vinson   3-26-1025 – 9-19-1982[1]

Elsie Ethel Vinson Carpenter 2-15-1924–4-28-1989[1]

Gary Bulen Vinson   2-16-1946 – 3-31-2005[1]

Stella Jean Carpenter   6-25-1946 – Unknown[1]

Allen Tipton St. Clair, Sr.   2-25-1922 – 10-10-1075[1]

Herman Lee St. Clair   10-29-1926 – 8-19-1981[1]

Ruby Edith Akins St. Clair   10-29-1926 – 8-19-1981[1]

James Howry St. Clair   5-27 1924 – 6-1986[1]

George Jackson St. Clair   5-27-1924 - 4-25-1991[1]

Sylvia Gay St. Clair Clower   1-19-1935 – 12-5-1994[1]

Ralph David St. Clair   2-17-1932 – 3-19-2001[1]

Allen Tipton St. Clair, Jr.   7-12-1944 – 12-20-2007[1]

Johnny Archie St. Clair   7-7-1017 – 2-1-2002[1]

Toy Marie Early St. Clair   12-26-1927 -- Unknown[1]

FRIENDS, NEIGHBORS AND TEACHERS

General Lee Jones   6-26-1898 – 2-4-1986[2]

Rosa Mae Keever Jones   3-1-1906 – 1996[2]

Wiley Candler Jones   10-28-1927--1-15-1995[2]

Frankie Lee Jones Gootie   8-2601940 -- 1-2-1994[2]

William Raleigh Bingham   5-30-1892 --- 7-26-1984[3]

Lola Bates Bingham   9-1-1909 --- 5-3-1977[3]

Paul Ledford   Unknown

Edith S. Hemphill   1895 -- Unknown[4]

Jean Smoak Hemphill   5-30-1920 – 2-18-1993[4]

Harry Moses	Unknown

CLASSMATES FRANKLIN HIGH CLASS OF 1964

Classmate	Year of passing
Bill Givens	1979
Helton Sanders	1981
Ronnie "Bo" Bolton	1986
L. T. Gibson	1987
Stanley Marvin	1999
Teresa Calison Brown	1999
Robbie Gibson	2000
Pam Cunningham Shirley	2000
Robert Dalton	2001
Jo Evelyn Barnard	2002
Jackie Carpenter	2002
Lawrence Cook	2003
Shirley Kell Moore	2003
Ila Sue Blaine	2003
Lee McGlamery	2003

Arland Evitt	2004
Carol Worst Larsen	2004
Shirley Woodard Guyer	2004
Janie Hooper Matthews	2004
Max Cunningham	2006
Glenda Henderson Cook	2007
Joyce Elliott	2007
Butch Malonee	2008

List Source[5]

Introduction

I invite you to travel with me back to a simpler, more respectful place and time — in the Southern Blue Ridge Mountains, in a day in which a little could go much farther and persons were not judged by the size of their bank accounts. A time when one's word was his or her bond.

To me, my childhood was very endearing because I was made to feel special by parents who cared deeply about me and my well-being. From my earliest recollection I learned invaluable lessons which would carry me through the complexities of life, both good and bad.

Go with me now to the cabin of my youth. Explore with me a mysterious place where I was able to discern the harsh reality of the world which lay ahead — beyond the thistle patch.

Chapter One

It was July 2001, and my wife and I had stopped by to see the little cabin on Blaine Branch. This tiny historic log home had been the nest of my impressionable years, and flooded my being with countless memories which would indelibly form my views of life. The old gravel road which I recalled so well had now been paved.

"Hey, which one of Paul Ledford's sons are you?"

"Stanley! Stanley St. Clair! Is that really you? I haven't seen you in a coon's age. How ya been gettin' along? I'm Bud."

"I'm doing fine. My mom passed away last year and she was buried beside my dad out at Tessentee. We come up every year to decorate the graves."

"Sorry about your mother. How old was she?"

"She was ninety. Would have been ninety-one last August. How many of you live here on the old farm now?"

"Just me and my boys and my sister, Amie Sue. She lives in the house you can see across the road up the lane. You know Whig died several years back. The others still live around the area."

"We stopped by to see the old home place. Your folks lived in the old house for a while, didn't they?"

"Yeah. But they both passed away, too."

"I know. And the Binghams are gone. But some of the Joneses are still around. I've seen some of them."

"Yeah, The Binghams, of course, passed away some time ago. And the older Joneses. Wiley and Hazel built a house over in the curve across from where his dad lived. Wiley died a few years ago. Their kids live around here. Nancy lived in Michigan for many years, now she lives over on the hill. This valley's full of different folks now. Some of 'em from Florida. They've put up a bunch of new homes. We built this house several years ago, me and my wife. My son, Mike, is gettin' ready to build over where the old house is settin'. We got it sold to a man who's buildin' a pioneer village somewhere down in Florida. I think I've got his card...Yeah, here it is; you can have it. Call this guy. He wanted to know more about the history of the old house than we could tell him."

"How much did he give you for it?"

"Twelve hundred dollars."

"Is that all? I would have given you that much! I wish I had known it!"

But it was actually a few years later before the little cabin was torn down, log by log, and hauled away. And I never even called the man on the card.

My first look at the little log cabin on Blaine Branch was one sunny morning in early June, 1954. As our green Chevy half-ton pickup, strained by the heavy trailer it was pulling, topped the hill overlooking that fairest-of-valleys, my heart flew out the window. I had already fallen in love with the home of my youth. I was only seven, soon to be eight. But it seemed that I could do no wrong in the eyes of my parents when I was that age.

"Marvin! You look like you haven't eaten in weeks. You're thin as a rail!"

"Oh, good day, Darling! You worry too much about me. I'm fine. I've been busy tryin' to fix the place up, gettin' ready for you and Stanley."

"Yes, I worry about you! And no wonder. Well, I'm here now, and you won't go hungry. It's a good thing you didn't come down early last year when you bought the place."

"Son! Come here! I have something for you!" Daddy said, trying not to pay heed to my mother's concern.

I reached up and hugged my dad. "What did you get me?"

"See. It's a bag of marbles. The big one's called a dough-roller. You'll have a lot of fun with them. I got you a model airplane, too."

"Oh, boy!" They were cat's eyes. Clear with a colored streak in the center.

"Cockadoodle-do-o-o!" A colorful cocky Bantam rooster flapped his wings rapidly as if to let us know that he was in charge.

"I've already got several chickens, some hogs, a cow and a mule."

"What does the mule do, Daddy?"

"Oh, he plows the fields. See those little stalks comin' up out there? I plowed and planted five acres of corn this year. We'll have plenty of corn to feed our chickens and make feed for the cow. And we've got apple trees and a thicket of plum trees up by the barn. And there are fox grapes growin' between the meadows. This is a great little farm."

"You said the *mule* plowed the fields, Daddy!" I laughed. It seemed my thoughts got frozen on the mule.

"Yeah, he does, but I hold the plow and keep him in the rows. We kinda do it together."

I nodded and wiped my sweaty forehead.

"Let's get the trailer parked and the truck unloaded, Marvin," Mama said with a tiny frown. "Jess has driven us all the way down here to North Carolina from Ohio. We're tired, and I'm sure he'll want to get home to Rabun Gap and rest."

"Sure, Darling."

I heard a high-pitched squeal and dashed around the cabin. A bristly reddish-brown sow was chasing a black-and-white-spotted one away from a rough wooden trough in the fenced hog lot. Her teeth were showing her angry displeasure.

The little cabin, fronted by majestic walnut trees, sat back about forty-five feet from the dusty gravel road which meandered along Blaine Branch in the Patton Community of Macon County. Five road miles sep-arated the scenic farm from the historic town of Franklin.

My father, Marvin Woodrow St. Clair, had met my mother, Trula Vinson, in early 1945 through his chummy relationship with her brother, Rowe, with whom he worked at the Hercules Powder Plant in Radford, Virginia, near his childhood home in Christiansburg. It had been my Uncle Rowe who had first lived there, and had sold the farm to my parents.

My dad had served two adventure-filled years in the Civilian Conservation Corp, in Waynesboro, Virginia. There he had been introduced to acting because of his well-developed physique, great strength and chiseled features. He had played an Indian scout in a second-rate movie titled "The Fighting Kentuckians" in the summer of 1938, which utilized a number of locals. But he had impressed the producers to such a degree that he had been offered a contract to travel to Hollywood as a regular with the company.

In extracurricular sports activities, the CCC base had also offered boxing. He had been trained by none other than Jack Blackburn, the original trainer of the great Joe Lewis. His expertise in this endeavor, coupled with the fact that in sparring he knocked Blackburn out, led to another tempting offer for a career as a heavyweight pro boxer.

Having recently lost his father, my dad had immense respect for his saintly mother, and refused to buck her will when she asked him to nix both career proposals.

He had then enlisted in the Navy when US involvement in World War II began and had disappointingly been sent home from his ship due to problems with an injury he had sustained in the CCCs.

My mom's family had journeyed west to take up a homestead in the rugged Bighorn Mountains of Montana when she was only six years of age. After obtaining a diploma in "Normal Training" in 1930, she had begun a teaching career in a one-room schoolhouse in Sheridan, Wyoming. Her next term had been in Harrison, Arkansas, along the road back home.

Upon the family's return to North Carolina in the late '30s, she had attended Perry Business College in Georgia and traveled throughout the South preparing wives of servicemen abroad to qualify them for careers in business. Then, after teaching an impressive number of illiterate adults to read and write, for which she was recognized by *Who's Who in North Carolina Education*", she had served as an instructor for one term at what was to become Lee University in East Tennessee.

That night, as we sat in the front room of our little cabin after the evening meal, my father excitedly related his adventures since arriving and his ambitious plans for the farm.

"Son, there are deer around here, and lots of squirrels and rabbits. We'll go hunting this fall and winter, you and me. I'll teach you all about the trees and plants — how to find what you need to get by in the woods, and how to farm. We'll have a good time here on our little place. We've got about eighty acres, more or less. It goes on both sides of the road, and up these mountains!'

"That's great, Daddy. You can show me plenty of stuff. I'm getting sleepy. Where will I sleep?"

"Well, right now we'll all stay in our bedroom. Look back here, You see this pantry? This is where your mama will keep the food. See that ladder?"

"Uh-huh. What's up there?"

"Well, it goes up in the attic. We can fix you a bedroom up there when you get used to the place."

"I'm a big boy, Daddy. I'm not afraid. I can sleep up there."

"Okay, we'll fix your room real soon."

I opened my mouth in a big yawn, and stretched my arms toward the rafters, my eyes heavy with sleep.

Marvin in the CCC Camp at age 19

Chapter Two

"You'll have chores every day. Once your chores are done, you can play."

"What are chores, Mama?"

"Chores are tasks which you must complete to help your daddy and me on the farm."

"What do you want me to do?"

"There will be several chores. Some in the morning, some in the evening. First thing every morning, as soon as you get up, you'll go out and feed the chickens. They get up at daylight and need to eat to start their day. Your daddy will show you where the corn is. He'll also show you the other things you need to do to help him."

"Come on, Son, I'll show you now. I already fed 'em this morning. We let you sleep late because you were so tired last night. But that was the last time."

My chores, I soon was to discover, included gathering eggs, slopping hogs, weeding the garden, and helping at milking time. But the pleasure was all mine. Also, water must be fetched from the spring. To reach this gelid source of life necessitated walking across the road and over a narrow one-plank bridge crossing Blaine Branch, a tributary of Cartoogechaye Creek, then along a path about twenty feet farther. This water was used for all of our needs from drinking to cooking and bathing and washing our clothes. Mama kept her ringer-type washing machine on the front porch, which resulted in frequent freezing of clothing during the winter months. Our clothes were hung on a plastic-coated clotheslines stretched tautly between the trees, and attached by two types of pens—one's with round heads which were one-piece, and those with two conjoined sides clasped together with springs. Either way, we had to hang the shirts and blouses by the bottoms, and the pants and skirts by the tops. Again, utilization of the simplicities was what made life in the golden fifties so special.

The box-like mobile home which had accompanied us from Casey's Trailer Park at 4001 Navarre Rd, S.W., Canton, Ohio, was a hand-crafted, one-of-a-kind structure. It had been lovingly designed and built by my family's dearest friend, Steve Manco, who had thrown in for free a forties-model television—a large square wooden box with a small circular screen. I felt like a privileged character. Now I could sit glued to this magical machine on Saturday mornings after adjusting the antenna which was attached to the end of the cabin, and put myself into the adventures of

Roy Rogers, Gene Autry, the Cisco Kid and Hopalong Cassidy! After my chores were finished and breakfast at the table had been completed, of course.

The trailer just sat there, parallel to the end of our cabin, for many years without an occupant.

My father had made his rounds in the community immediately after making the move early that year. Just above us at the end of the road was the grey-weathered home of Mr. Raleigh Bingham and his slender second wife, Lola.[3] Between the Binghams and our cabin was another antique dwelling — that of Mr. Binghams' daughter, Maude, her hubby, Raleigh Hopkins, and their four children. The eldest, Mary, was a year my junior, and the other three were as stair-steps; first, John, then Ethel and Emma.

On the way out of the valley, on the hill, the next asbestos-shingled home was that of Wiley Jones, his spouse, Hazel, and their offspring, Rachel and Wayne. Living with them was Hazel's father, Thomas Buchannan.[2]

Next, around a pleasant curve, sat the white, thirties-style home of Wiley's parents, General Lee and Rosa Mae Jones and their daughters, Frankie and Nancy. With them dwelt General Jones' eighty-seven-year-old mom, Laura Ellen.[2]

It was a scorching summer day and Mama was dabbing her head with a handkerchief while listening to Our Miss Brooks on the radio. She had just made up a pitcher of black cherry Kool-Aid. Daddy was in the field, and she had asked me to carry him out a mason jar full. An army-green station wagon pulled up in our drive. As usual when a strange vehicle showed up I was ogling. There were some words painted on the car's door.

"Mama, there's somebody out there."

"I'm not deaf, Son. I heard the car pull up. Go out and see who it is."

"Hey there, young man," the smiling stranger sang out. "Is your mother around?"

"Sure, mister," I said, nodding. "Who are you?"

"I'm the Watkins man. I have a lot of things ladies need. Just tell your mother I'm here. She'll know."

By this time Mama had placed the pitcher of Kool-Aid in the refrigerator and was walking out to greet our visitor.

"Hello, I've been hoping you'd stop by to see me. Mrs. Jones said you had a route out here. I'm Trula St. Clair." My mother extended her hand.

"George Allen, good to meet ya."

"Do you have vanilla flavoring?"

"Of course. And several others. Most ladies also like our salve and lotions."

"I guess I could try a tin of your salve. My son is always getting cuts and scrapes. I'll take the vanilla, too. "

"Don't you want to try the walnut?"

"No, sir. Maybe next time. Money doesn't grow on trees, you know."

"Yes, ma'am. That'll be $1.25 total."

"Whew! Can't stand much of those prices!"

"I'm sure you'll see the value once you use our fine products."

"I hope so. Thank you, sir."

And she did. My mother became a regular Watkins customer.

The summer flew by, as always when one is having fun. During the days I would venture out and explore my surroundings…a little more each time.

One sunny Monday afternoon I had been hanging around with my father as he ate his lunch in the shade by the cornfield, asking probing questions as curious children of that age are prone to do. As Daddy returned to hoeing the weeds from the hardened hills of corn, I pushed my skinny form between the strands of barbed wire which separated the cornfield from the section of woods behind it and stepped out toward my newest adventure. Rambling onward, I could hear the faint song of a distant whippoorwill. I followed that lonely voice deeper into the forest and over a peaceful rolling knoll. I was nearing a great upward hill. Suddenly, the trees became sparser, and the light of the glorious sun seemed to flood in around me—I was entering a clearing where rocks were stacked about as if to form a wall or a fence. But something else caught my eye. A patch of purple-blooming thorny weed-like flowers were growing there. I'd never seen anything like them before. Well, it seemed like I may have seen one or two of them, but never a sight like this! They certainly weren't among the plants Daddy had shown me so far. He had pointed out something similar that were nightshades or something. And he had mentioned jimson weeds that cows eat. But what were these? Carefully I picked one of the sharp blooms. Somehow I felt that I should go no farther, so I carefully headed back. One thing my dad had already taught me well: how to mark my way and get home.

When I arrived at the field, I ran to my dad and threw my little arms around his damp, sweaty pant legs. My loving dad looked down at me, laid the hoe at his side and hugged me.

"What is this, Daddy?' I asked, thrusting the bloom upward.

My dad laughed that hearty laugh that made him who he was.

"That's a thistle, Son. You must have found the thistle patch way back by the big mountain. Don't go back there. You're goin' a bit too far away for a little fellow. No tellin' what you might find back there."

"Like what, Daddy?'

"Well, that's not on our place. There's no fence to show some of these property lines. You see, there used to be a shack out there. And, well, let's just say everything that was there has been moved. I don't know where, and I don't want to, but I don't want you goin' beyond the thistle patch."

"Why, Daddy?"

"Haven't you asked enough questions for one day when you were here at lunch time?"

I ducked my head and dashed toward home. But I couldn't help but wonder what was out there — beyond the thistle patch.

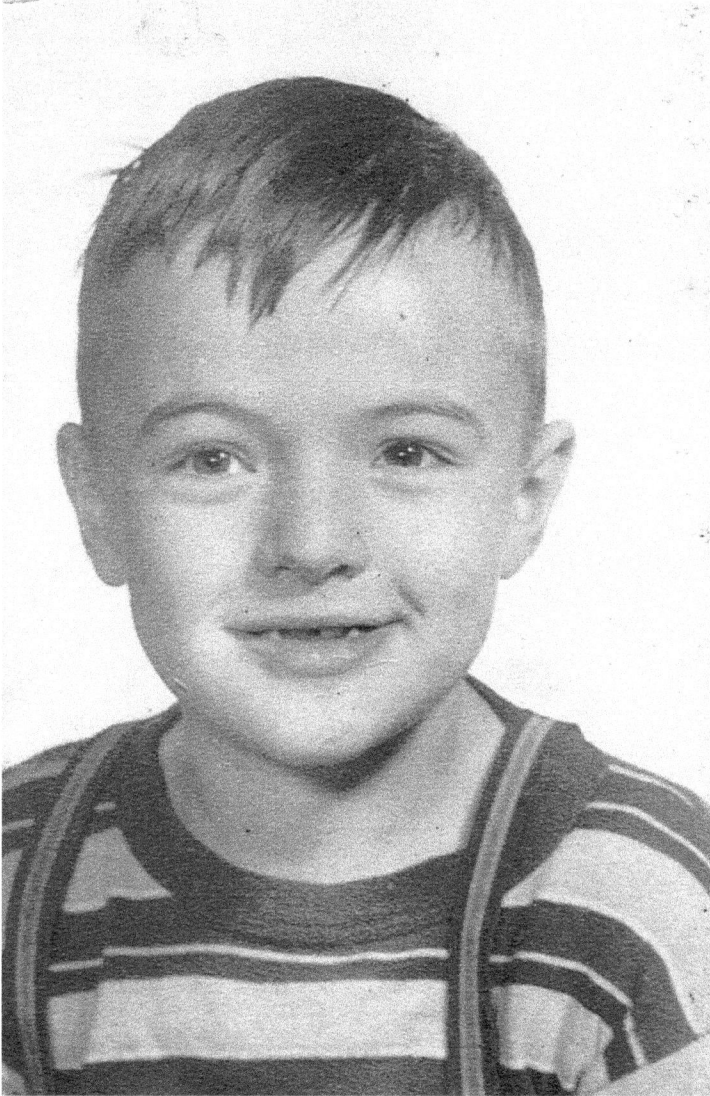

A look back – Stanley in grade one

Chapter Three

My eighth birthday came and went. In early September, right after Labor Day, I would be boarding the big yellow bus that Mr. Dills drove to travel to Franklin Elementary and enroll in third grade. When school began I became well acquainted with the kids around our community.

"Hi, I'm Nancy."

"I'm Stanley. I live over the hill in the little log house."

"Yeah, I know," Nancy said with a giggle. "The big girl that went to the back is my sister, Frankie."

"It's good to meet you. What grade are you in?"

"Third."

"Me, too. Just follow me when we get to school."

"Sounds good to me."

And I did. Having someone who knew her way helped.

Wayne and Rachel Jones were still very small, as were most of the Hopkins children, but Mary Hopkins, I learned soon, was in second grade that year, and soon became friendly as well.

My teacher that first term was Miss Meadows, an easy-going, slim young lady with lovely dark hair and eyes.

"Class, this is Stanley St. Clair. He's new here. He and his parents moved to the area this summer from Ohio."

"Are you a Yankee?" a tiny voice said.

I raised my eyebrows. "My mama's family is from around here. My daddy is from Virginia. I was born just down the road in Clayton, so I'm *not* a Yankee!" Somehow I didn't realize what a difference the Civil War had made and that its affects were still being felt after ninety years in the South. But I knew that a "Yankee" was somebody from the North and that it seemed to mean something bad in the South.

I heard a giggle and looked into the eyes of a cute slim blonde named Peggy. My mind raced to the little redhead named Roxie that I thought was so pretty in Mrs. Vance's class the year before. But I wasn't ready to think about girls.

I took well to my new school, although I missed the busier activities of Prairie College Elementary in Canton, Ohio, where I had grown accustomed to special teachers coming in for music and art. My art instructor the past two years had been Mr. Gurley, a stout-built, kind soul who patiently taught me how to form the basics of the human body and still life at the tender age of six.

My articulate mother had tutored me in printing, reading and reciting an extensive repertoire of nursery rhymes at two years of age. Before a day of public schooling she was determined that I could be equipped for life.

The school at Franklin was sprawled across the height of a red-clay-based hill, above a leveled crater where the old high school had burned. A new one was being constructed. Behind the school, a slope dropped rapidly. This hill contained a labyrinth of paths wandering through a forest containing tangled grape vines and pesky kudzu. At the end of the matted mess, a fence separated the woods from the local drive-in movie theater. Though strictly off-limits for school children, it was not unusual to find one exploring there.

In my third grade classroom I would first come to know a number of little persons with which I would retain bonds throughout the years.

Though all summer we benefitted from our labors in the garden, in September and October the first harvest was being taken in. Pumpkins, corn and cornfield beans. This glorious impression would inspire my poem, Mom's Heart, one which would later be accepted by Ideals Magazine, and appear in my volume of poetry published in 2010, "Reflections on Life".

I have made this poem a part of this book.

MOM'S HEART

The year was 'fifty-four,

The sky, October blue.

The house was logs and boards,

But love flowed through and through.

The yard was raked

With piles of leaves,

And pumpkins filled the porch.

The fireplace held a cozy flame,

But Mom's heart held a torch.

The lady was a beam of light

Wherever she would go.

No need to say Mom was a gem,

To meet her was to know.

"♫ Fair thee well, fair thee well, fair thee well my fairy Fay! Singin' polly wolly doodle, singin' polly wolly, singin' polly wolly doodle all the day! ♪"

"You seem happy this morning, Daddy," I said. It was a bright day in late September and the sun was smiling over Western North Carolina.

"Yeah, Son, I'm happy because we're going to rake up the hay today that I cut last week and put it in the barn loft. Make hay while the sun's shinin' as the sayin' goes! You can be a big help. We'll get started right after breakfast."

"What's that stuff you're mixing up, Mama?" I asked, glancing at the table. "It looks like coffee."

"It's Postum, Son. You know I don't drink coffee, and I sure wouldn't let you have any. 'Of milk and water, drink you a plenty, but not tea or coffee until you are twenty!'"

"What's Postum, Mama?"

"It's a safe hot drink that we all can enjoy that tastes something like coffee, but doesn't have any caffeine in it. And before you ask, caffeine is something that makes folks nervous and keeps them awake at night."

"Oh. Can I taste the Postum?"

"Sure. You can drink it with your oatmeal for breakfast."

"Hmmm...I guess that tastes okay. At least it's hot. Thank you, Mama."

"You're welcome, Son. Now eat your cereal so you can be strong and help your daddy. Oatmeal will stick to your ribs."

"Why does it need to be on my ribs?"

"That just means it stays with you and doesn't give out in the middle of the day. Now don't ask so many questions and eat!"

Daddy drove the truck into the upper meadow which was streaked with windrows of greenish-golden hay, and parked it.

"Here's where we start."

We both got out and Daddy handed me a pitchfork — one with a short handle and a circular metal grip.

Together we began thrusting the forks into wind-rows and loading the truck. After it was full and running over each time, we would transport it to the barn and I would climb the ladder into the loft and move the hay forward as my father would pitch it in.

The day was one of enjoyable working together with my loving dad. One which, though many other days together would follow, would go down in the annals of my pleasurable childhood memoirs.

When I first met my Aunt Blanche, Uncle Steve's spouse, I had a cute story I just had to relate to her. I had recently read it in Boy's Life Magazine.

A country girl named Jessie had gone away to the city to college. When she told her roommate her name, she roused quite a chuckle.

"You need to change it to Jessica! That's much more modern and hip," she was informed.

And so, the country girl became Jessica. Upon writing home, she informed her parents of her decision, and asked respectfully to be referred to in the future by her modern name.

The parents were quite taken aback, and decided to play along with a humorous illustration which might show their upstart daughter the error of her ways. Their letter read:

Dear Jessica,

We are so pleased that you want to be accepted by your peers.

Our cowica had a calfica, and if it was a girlica we were going to call her Bossica, but it was a boyica, so we decided to call him Samica.

Love,

Momica and Dadica

The story was such a hit, that every time I met a new family member afterward, my mother insisted that I tell that traditional little yarn.

It was a Saturday and we had gone to Franklin to do our shopping. First we went to the Winn-Dixie so Mama could get S&H Green Stamps with her groceries. These were stuck in books which could eventually be cashed in for fabulous prizes. She was also accumulating sections of the Webster's new Unabridged Dictionary for me to use with my homework. When complete it would become a phenomenal volume which would exceed a thousand pages. Then we had stopped at the five-and-ten for some thread. Now my mother and I had just come out of the Salvation Army Thrift Store on Palmer Street, and had walked into the fruit stand next door to look around. Our garden had played out by that time of year. As luck would have it, they also carried candy bars and it was past my lunch time. I noticed that a new brand of bar was just out and being offered at a special price! Candy bars sold back then for five cents each, and this new one—a Zero Bar—a brown chocolate nugget coated with a white chocolate frosting, was only three cents! And I had a penny which was burning a hole in my pocket.

"Mama," I said, tugging on her jacket tail, "do you have two cents? I'm hungry and there is a new candy bar here for only three cents."

Now I knew that money was short and that my mother had skimped and cut coupons to get the groceries that week. I just didn't know how nearly broke she really was. My dear mother scraped through her pocket book, searching desperately for cash of any denomination. First she found one cent, and finally, another.

"Here, Son. This is all I've got, but you can have it."

Tears flooded my little eyes. "Are you sure, Mama?"

"Of course. Whenever I have anything, you can have it if you need it."

And she meant it. That's the kind of mother she was.

But that October brought one of the worst tragedies that would ever befall our family. My uncle, Steve, who had been hunting, came home to his house on Highway 23 in the "Longview stretch", and hung his rifle on the wall. He thought that he had taken all of the remaining ammunition out of the clip. His oldest son, Alvin, who was only three years and seven months old, was playing in the room adjacent to where the gun was hanging. Somehow he jarred the wall, and the rifle fell, striking the floor in such a way as to cause it to fire—directly through the wall and into Alvin, instantly taking his precious young life. This was such a freak accident that no one could fathom exactly how it could have occurred.

That was the first funeral I can recall attending. The little church where the sad service was held was beside the cemetery where his tiny body would be laid to rest. This would be the first in a string of family burials which would be held at Tessentee.

One day that year a black-and-white-spotted male Shepherd dog showed up at our little cabin. He was obviously hungry. And he was limping.

"Daddy! This dog has been hurt. His left hind paw is partly cut off!" I exclaimed.

"Looks like he was caught in a bear trap."

"Here, boy. Have a bone. It's got a little meat left on it," Mama said.

"Great! That means I can keep him, then?'

"If it's alright with your daddy, and you'll feed him. If no one claims him, I guess I don't care."

I looked up into my dad's steel-grey eyes. He couldn't say no.

"I can get scraps for him where I pick up hog feed at the grocery stores," Daddy added.

Fall also became a time for me to accompany my dad into the magical forest and learn the art of hunting. I was soon very familiar with the many native trees and plants, survival techniques, and how to locate and kill rabbits and squirrels. Of course I was not yet permitted to carry a gun. I had named my dog "Rover", and he had proved invaluable as a hunter and companion.

But sometimes I just enjoyed staying in and drawing or working on the stamp collection which I had begun by steaming the postage off of the letters which had come in the mail. I made a smooth wooden cover for them, engraved "Stamps" and the date on it with my pocket knife, polished it and tied it neatly together with a shoe string.

Life in the country was good.

Marvin and Stanley with Reddy and Stubby

Chapter Four

The promised bed was prepared for me in the loft, over the front room/kitchen, but in the chilling months of winter the frigid breezes often blew blankets of snow through the crack along the cap of the roof to obscure my top quilt, and upon awakening I would shake off and sweep away my uninvited cover. A six to seven inch snow was not uncommon.

Before third grade was ended, I was already helping my dad plant corn for the next season. Corn served a variety of significant purposes. Early soft specimens were plucked for roasting ears, then, when harvest rolled around, well-developed grain would be stored for seed. Next, some would be taken to the mill and ground for meal. Cornbread was made tastier by adding "cracklings" to the dough. These crunchy morsels were bits of pork from a neighborhood hog killing, a synergic event which brought all of the farmers together to share in both the labor and the rewards thereof. Corn also was used to mix with molasses and chopped hay for cattle feed, and was excellent for our foul. We now had two cows, Daisy, a Guernsey, and Rose, a Hereford. Each year at least one calf would be born to each of them. Not only did we have a variety of chicken breeds, but my dad had now added a small flock of squawking guineas. Those which chose not to enter the chicken houses would roost on the limbs of the trees in our backyard. Not only guineas, but chickens as well. Eventually, my father clipped one wing on each renegade to keep them from flying into the trees to roost.

Each of the chickens had been given names by my mother. Two of the hens were Faith and Hope, and a Leghorn rooster was named Charity. Another speck-led Game hen was called Shangri-La. As more roosters were added to our flock it became a necessity to break up the cock fights that would sporadically take place, but somehow we were able to keep them from annihilating each other.

"It's coming spring, Son. We must set some of the hens so we can raise some chicks. The pullets will grow into laying hens, and the young roosters will soon be good for frying," my mother said.

And, so, each year in mid February, about the time of planting root crops like onions, turnips, sweet pota-toes and radishes, we would begin to select hens to set and our flock grew immensely. My dad would sell the large eggs, both light-shelled Leghorn eggs, and the dark ones from the Rhode Island Reds and Domineckers. We were only permitted to eat the Bantam eggs, and the double-yolked ones. These did not fit the normal standard for sale. Also sold on my father's in-town route during the proper season were blackberries, which grew in wild abundance around the swamp below the cabin.

The little log house on Blaine Branch had stood proudly for over one hundred years, having origi- nally been held together by mud and wooden pegs, which were still intact. It was the old home place of the Blaine Family, the maternal grandparents of long- time Macon County Register of Deeds, Lake V. Shope. His parents, Zeb and Melvina Blaine Shope, had been married in that cabin on Christmas day, 1898. From there they had crossed the mountain to spend the night.[6]

During the thirties, we were told, a man had been killed in the house—rumor had it that he was shot through the front room door by a jealous husband, and that his ghost still roamed the house at night, and chains dragged from his arms and legs. But strangely enough, my family and I never heard or saw any sign of this phantom.

The entire cabin consisted of two rooms connected by a duel-faced fireplace capped on the front by an open vestibule, and on the rear by a pantry. Above was only the loft. The aluminum roof had been put on by my grandfather, Ansel "Pop" Vinson in 1948. At one time a kitchen had been added in back, but it no longer stood. Underneath, a root cellar was burrowed which made room for buried potatoes and was lined with shelves on which my mother would pack dozens of jars filled with cooked berries, fruit and vegetables. Always more than we needed in the event of a poor growing season. Having been reared in an age of uncertainty and scarcity, she felt that she could never plan too well.

My uncle, Rowe Vinson, who had begun his family there, had remained for the time being in Canton, Ohio, and still lived at the mobile home park where we had moved after leaving the large two-story home downtown on Fifteenth Street.

"Ain't you afraid to sleep in that haunted house, Stanley?" John Hopkins asked me one day while he and his sisters were visiting me.

"No, John," I said. "I don't believe in ghosts, and I've never heard any noises at night!"

"'ell I wouldn't sleep there! They is ghosts. Believe me."

John was very small at the time, and he had definitely heard something. The scary tales of someone wanting him to stay home at night.

The first work I did away from home was for a couple who lived on the main Patton Community Road coming in from town. The man's name was Jim Liner. My dad had become acquainted with them previously. The Liners finally met me when we all stopped by their neat white house one summer day that year I was to become nine. They told me that they had a nice dress suit about my size. I think they would have been happy to give it to me, but my parents preferred that I work and earn it. It was arranged that my father bring me by one Saturday and leave me to pick beans. Once the job was done, I was presented with the first suit of clothes I had ever owned. My mother proudly altered the sleeves of the jacket, and the legs of the pants. I will never forget that little sky-blue suit. Now, on dress-up occasions, I was as sharp as the richest of them.

In those early days in our new home, we didn't go to church anywhere, so occasionally I walked by myself to Patton Methodist Church, about a mile away at the junction of our road with Patton Road, the "hard service" highway. One thing that attracted me was the fact that they had a Cub Scout troop meeting there. I asked my parents for permission to join, and to my surprise, they were delighted for me to take part, though as it turned out, I didn't remain a member of the group for very long.

My mother sold what were known in those days as "mottos". Today there are much more ornate examples in Wal-Mart. But these were heavy cardboard, and were navy blue with either a Bible verse or a catchy saying etched on them in silvery metallic letters. Things like "Home Sweet Home" or "The Family Who Prays Together Stays Together". And the lettering usually had colorful flowers around it. Many folk would hang them on their walls as they were, while others would select frames for them. This was done door-to-door in better homes throughout the area. She also sold greeting cards for special occasions like birthdays or holidays. Already she was taking me with her and teaching me to sell them.

In spring of 1956 a huge thrill in the Franklin area came from local filming of sequences of Walt Disney's classic *The Great Locomotive Chase* on the abandoned Tallulah Falls Railway. This film was based on the true story of Anderson's raid, a military maneuver on April 12th, 1862 in Northern Georgia in which Union volunteers commandeered a rebel train, "the General", and ran it north toward Chattanooga.[7] The premier of the movie in Franklin on June 8th caused quite a stir.

I will never forget the day my uncle, Steve Vinson, took me out on his brother Dan's farm and showed me a caboose in which Fess Parker was reportedly staying during parts of the filming.

Then in October of that year, the epic motion picture, The Ten Commandments, was released. My parents, though conscientious Christians, didn't forbid me to attend movies. At times I would go to the downtown theater and see an acceptable film. For some reason we hadn't seen *The Great Locomotive Chase*, though. I know I saw *Bambi*, *Davy Crocket* and *Joan of Arc*. But *The Ten Commandments*! This was definitely a family affair. Daddy drove us to the drive in and we were mesmerized by Cecil B. DeMille's sweeping cinematic masterpiece. It seemed that we were right there with Moses when the Children of Israel crossed the Red Sea on dry land.

That year brought another new adventure which would change my life. Uncle Rowe and his wife were divorced and he and his six children returned to the area around Macon County, North Carolina and neighboring Rabun County, Georgia. By this time my grandparents were in Rabun County. That large a family was a bit more than Uncle Rowe could care for on his own.

I had turned ten that August, and welcomed the fact that some of the Vinson boys would be staying with us. Room was made in the sleeping loft, and Gary and Mike become like brothers to me. Gary was six months my senior, and Mike, seven months my junior. So we three grew close in spite of obvious personality differences. Gary and I were in Mrs. Hemphill's fifth grade class; Mike, in Mrs. Jamieson's fourth grade.

Now, with playmates, I could really get use out of the marbles my dad had given me, and I began to collect more.

"We need to form a club," Gary said one day in early fall.

"Sounds good to me," I agreed.

"And we need to make up our own language so adults won't know what we're talking about."

"What about pig Latin?" Mike asked. E-way all-ay eady-ray ow-nay at-thay."

"They might figure that out," Gary protested. "We can come up with words which remind us of what we are trying to say."

"Like what?" I said.

"Like 'yeah' sounds a little like yellow. Instead of saying yellow we could say 'gold'. They'd never figure stuff like that out."

"Sounds great!" I laughed. "Gold. I think we should go for it."

"And we all need new names," Gary said with a mischievous smirk.

"We could call Stanley 'Stamo'," Mike said.

"And I can be 'Geronimo'." Gary was raising his clinched fist and shaking his forearm. "Or you can just call me 'Gary the Great'."

"And how about 'Micko' for Mike?'

"We can call it the plub! And we need a village," Gary said.

"Let's go across the road up the other side of the little branch that comes out of the mountain," I said. "There's a nice spot there up against the hill. We can build it out of small trees. I'll get Daddy's axe."

A tiny brook ran peacefully along that serene hillside and flowed downward past the spring and into Blaine Branch. Among the pebbles we would search for crawfish, which we knew as "craw-dads" and barbeque them over an open campfire in the evenings. We also found an abundance of salamanders which were sold for fish bait. The three little huts which we so carefully and seriously built from slender alders each contained a base with a root protruding outward which could be pulled upward to destroy it in the event of enemy attack. Then the top was covered by small limbs and each was coated with a blanket of brown leaves, with only a square opening in one corner of the top for entering and exiting.

"What should we call this place?" Mike asked.

"Let's call it St. Clairsville," I suggested.

"I say we name it Vinsonville," Gary said smugly. "Let's vote on it!"

I looked at the hands. No surprise. Two to one for Vinsonville.

"Majority rules!" said Gary the Great. And so it went.

On a winter weekend one of my other cousins was visiting. While we were away and he was lounging in one of the huts, he decided to build a fire under the opening to keep warm. The dry leaves soon ignited, and Vinsonville went up in smoke. Luckily, *this time* we arrived in time to extinguish the flames and save the day. At a later date we would not be so fortunate.

Marvin and Stanley on load of hay on Chevy truck

Chapter Five

After that first year, another of the Vinson brothers would join us. Lonnie was just less than a year younger than Mike. When he learned of our mysterious "plub" he was determined to become a member. By this time we were holding our secret meetings in the corn crib which was attached to the barn on the hill above the house on the west.

"Let Lonnie in the plub," Mike said impatiently to his older brother.

"Not so fast," Gary said with a serious face. "I think he should be initiated."

"What should he do?" I asked.

"I've got it!" Gary exclaimed. "We'll make him eat a whole lemon without frowning."

"Without frownin'! How am I gonna do that?" Lonnie protested with all sincerity.

"Yep! If you wantta be in our plub and be taught our secret plub lingo, you have to eat a lemon."

About that time Skippy, our mascot yellow and white cat, pounced on a fleeting mouse. I started digging in the corn and uncovered a nest of tiny pink babies, not even old enough to have their eyes open.

"What are you gonna do with them?" Mike said with a wrinkle in his brow.

"Here, Skippy!" I said.

"Ooow! I can't look," little Lonnie said, turning away.

"Then how are you gonna eat a lemon?" I asked smugly.

"Well, he'll eat it or he won't get in the plub!" Gary squawked.

"Okay! Okay! I'll do it!" Lonnie said.

And he did. We sneaked one out of the refrigerator, and up to the crib. Lonnie stayed straight-faced during the entire ordeal. He was now an official member of our notorious plub.

When planting every spring, Daddy always read the almanac and was careful to plant each crop "by the signs". He never would have dreamed of planting when the zodiac was not in his favor.

By now Daddy had bought another mule to make a team. The first one had been a "Jack", or male, named

Jocko. This one was a "Jenny", or female, called Jane. Sometimes we boys would put halters on the mules and go for a ride around our farm or up the road to the Hopkins place and back.

Each spring Daddy would clear "new ground" by cutting down trees and grubbing up the stumps. In the summer when he plowed the fields with Jocko and Jane he would leave the cabin at the crack of dawn, taking a canteen or mason jar filled with water and a brown paper bag lunch. His shirt would always be soaking wet with perspiration by mid-morning, and he would keep plowing and yelling at those mules. He would only break once in the forenoon and once in the mid-afternoon for water, and when the blazing sun told him it was high noon, for lunch. Farming was his passion, and he was consumed by it.

About this time, Daddy was having trouble with his stomach. No wonder, with his brutal lifestyle. My mother had been told that goat milk was good for one's stomach. Her other cure-all was Alka-Seltzer. We all got that for everything from colds to stomach aches. But this wasn't curing my father's tummy, so Daddy agreed to get some goats. They could also eat the weeds and unwanted underbrush. He could kill two birds with one stone.

Our first goats were given the surprising names of Nanny and Billy, but there would be many more. And we boys had to learn to milk the nannies. The kids were so precious. We finally developed quite a flock. Most of them were white, but we had some gray and mottled ones as well.

During this time our hog herd was also multiplying. One summer we had 100 little pigs to take to market. The prominent sows were "Reddy", a Durock-Russian mix, "Spot", a Poland China, "Whitey", a large Yorkshire, and "Stubby", an O.I.C. (Ohio Improved Chesterwhite) with a nub of a tail.

Another way of disposing of weeds, especially those we hoed up in the garden, was to feed them to the hogs. They especially loved the water weeds which grew along the branch and the rag weeds.

When Whitey had a litter of about ten piglets, one was very small, and my mother felt that she would not be able to make it on her own.

"Mama, if you and Daddy will let me have her, I will take care of her."

Mama looked at Daddy. They knew I meant it.

"Sure," Daddy said. "She will be yours. But you have to feed her with a bottle several times a day. You will have to clean out her box. She is totally your responsibility."

"Oh, thank you, Daddy!"

"When she is big enough you can take her to market. Whatever she brings will be yours."

I did all that they asked. And it was a pleasure. I don't even remember what I named her, but I remember that I loved that cute little pig and hated to see her go.

Mules, Jocko and Jane, ridden by Stanley and Gary

John Hopkins, front

Chapter Six

I had been fond of art since my first grade art teacher, Mr. Gurley, got me keyed up. My father's brother, Ralph, had done artwork for a number of years, and my mother had even taken an art correspondence course. I loved her work, and began to dream at an early age of being a commercial artist. I sketched on blank sheets of paper at home, and occasionally on the edges of my school book pages.

Gary, it turned out, also was talented. He asked for the privilege of painting a picture of *Bambi* and his mother on our sheet-rock kitchen-front-room wall. To my consternation, he was granted his wish. It seemed that Gary had a winning way: the uncanny ability to make everything alright with whomever he wished to influence. A talent which comes in very handy when getting one's way as a child. But the picture was actually very good, and I didn't mind it after it was done. Perhaps I was a tad jealous of his handsome looks and his charming personality. Gary was what one might call "a born leader", though this trite expression is a misnomer.

As he entered puberty, girls noticed him before 90% of the other young teens. Gary and Mike stayed with us through three school terms. They were my fifth, sixth and seventh. Lonnie was there for two years, and older brother, Anthony, joined them during only a few months the last summer.

A lot transpired during those three enchanting years while my "bro-cuzes" (our coined plub word for our special relationship) were a part of our little family.

As I alluded to earlier, Blaine Branch ran through a swamp below our cabin This created the most perfect locale in which to dam it up and hollow out an oblong hole about ten feet in length and four feet wide in which to splash and enjoy a break from the steaming summer heat. A gigantic Wolf River apple tree dug its sappy roots into the soil between the ole swimming hole and the winding gravel road upon which all traffic—cars, trucks, bicycles and horse-drawn wagons must navigate through the dale. Sometimes I would clamber up those mighty branches and straddle one of them while sinking my teeth into that juicy yellow fruit.

"I call this 'Happy Valley'," my dad told me one sunny morning as the streams of daybreak crept over Coweta Mountain to our east.

"Why, Daddy?" I asked.

"Because living here makes me happy. When I was a boy I lived on a beautiful farm like this on Falling

Branch in Virginia. I had cousins around some, too. But of course I had my own brothers. My cousins were part of a rough family. Back many years ago some of them were outlaws. The women would load the guns and the men would rob trains."

"But your family didn't do that!" I protested, as if trying to clear our good family name.

"Oh, of course not. They were hard-working honest people. Those were distant cousins, and back in the old days. Back around the late eighteen hundreds."

In December of 1957, Wiley Jones knocked at our door.

"Marvin, you had a call from one of your brothers in Virginia. He wants you to call him back. He said it's urgent. I've got the number."

We didn't have a phone.

Daddy frowned and put on his coat and the dark brown ten-gallon Stetson he wore for everyday. His white one was reserved for dress-up occasions.

My mother was nervously pacing. "What do you think is wrong, Mama. I know something is wrong," I said softly.

"I'm afraid something is wrong with your Grandma St. Clair."

I could feel the warm moisture building in my eyes and creeping out onto my reddening cheeks.

Daddy was gone about thirty minutes, but it seemed like an hour or longer. During those anxious moments my mind ran back to the fading memories to which I still clung of the two years when we lived near her in Virginia. I had been four when we moved to Ohio. Her home had been an enchanting two-story white farm house setting in a pleasant ravine in the verdant valley of Falling Branch at the base of a mountain, in some ways not dissimilar to where we were now living in North Carolina. My father had built us a cabin nearby.

One sparkling spring morning the last year we were there, my "Grandma" had looked at me with her soft eyes smiling.

"I'm going strawberry picking up on the hill, and you're coming with me."

She handed me a flat-bottomed tin cup and told me to put my berries in it while she filled a gallon lard pale. As I picked, I occasionally dumped mine in with hers.

"What are we going to do with all these strawberries, Grandma?" I asked.

"We're gonna take 'em home and put cream and sugar on 'em and eat 'em a-a-l-l-l up!"

And we did just that.

As my thoughts returned to the sobering reality of the present, I heard the front door opening.

"That was Johnny. My mother's bad off. She's in the hospital and they don't know if she's going to live long. They want me to go up there."

"Of course, Marvin. You'll have to go. How will you get there? Are you going to drive the truck up there?"

"No, I'll take the bus. I'll leave the truck so you can have somebody use it to take you to town when you need to go. I don't know how long I'll have to be gone."

"I guess I need to get my driver's license. I just never did see any use for that. I've always had a man around."

"Maybe you do need to. I'll be back as soon as I can."

My grandmother had heart problems and severe diabetes. She died on January 2nd, 1958. The evening before, her countenance had suddenly appeared to brighten. Setting up in the bed, she suddenly exclaimed, "Look at those shiny people!"

The family felt that she had experienced a vision of angels. The following poem is also from my book, "Reflections on Life".

WHEN GRANDMA WENT

(Slightly altered for accuracy)

When Grandma went to meet the Lord,

I had eleven years.

My father at her side had stayed

with mix of smiles and tears.

Her lids had widened to a glare;

Her simper broadened to a grin,

"Look at those shiny men," she said,

then slumped upon her bed again.

That night she passed; he'd gone to rest,

but wakened from his sleep;

a voice so clear spoke to his soul,

"Your mother's home with me."

My aunt, Sylvia and "Grandma" St. Clair

Chapter Seven

"They need more caddies at the golf course in Franklin." It was a boy I knew at school named Guy.

"Do you think I can do it?" I asked.

"Sure. I can show you the ropes."

One thing I knew about Guy: he was cocky and assertive. If Guy said he could show me how, by granny, he could.

That summer of 1958, I went to the golf course and signed in. There was a daily sheet, and caddies were called to go out with golfers in the order they arrived. Sure enough, I learned to be an efficient caddy. I liked hanging around the swimming pool and playing cards for fun at the caddy shack, too. That first summer I earned enough to buy all of my school clothes and begin feeling independent.

I had just gotten my first transistor radio and rock music was king. I heard that Elvis Presley had enlisted in the army in Memphis on March 24[8], but it seemed to make his songs even more popular. But a rising new star was catching on like wildfire. His name was Buddy Holly!

I recall one day I went out with my dad on his egg route and had my transistor radio on. Daddy was visiting with his special friend, Will Shepherd, a fine gentleman of African descent with whom he could get carried away talking about their Biblical views. On the radio Buddy Holly and the Crickets were blasting out "♪ Peggy Sue, I love you, with a love so rare and true! My Peggy, my Peggy Sue. ♪ " I thought it was such a super song.

Johnny Cash was in a field of his own and I loved him. On the local station, WFSC, they had a challenge. The number one song nationwide on the country charts was also number one locally on the pop requests. It was Cash's immortal "Ballad of a Teenage Queen". If they received a given number of requests, they would play the song twice in a row. The lines were swamped with calls.

During this time, my mother's parents, whom I called "Mom and Pop Vinson", were living on a farm which Pop had purchased near Rabun Gap, Georgia, in the Wolf Fork Community. They lived close to the Gibbs family who had come with them from Arkansas. Uncle Jess and Aunt Lazelle, in the early years of their marriage, lived with them before building their new home in the valley below. All of us kids loved climbing the rock cliffs above the house. It seemed that we were oblivious to the dangers that could befall us if one of us were to fall from those steep, rocky walls which nature had formed there.

But the danger I actually experienced at Rabun Gap came not from high on the mountain, but from a far less expected, benign-seeming source. One day while I was yet eleven we were visiting with them.

"Trula," Aunt Lazelle said to my mother in a serious tone, "the well here is getting dangerously low. I don't know what we will do if it runs dry."

Mike and I overheard. As curious as we were, we made an on-the-spot executive plub decision to investigate this unfortunate bit of news. The well was adjacent to their home. Mike on one side, and I on the other, we proceeded to cautiously lift the massive concrete cover from the roof of the well. Mike apparently sensed a quiver on my side and naturally certain that I had lost my grip, he relinquished his claim to his burden. The entire weight of that gigantic dome was instantly transferred to my side, severing the tip of my right middle finger, and slicing profusely its match. I spent that night in the new hospital at Clayton. Miraculously the fingertip had dangled by a particle of skin, and was able to be reattached. Sadly, both a house door and a car door were slammed on it while I was attempting to recover. This unfortunate accident was no one's fault — merely the result of the curious nature of two playful children.

But that was not the only scars I received as a pre-teen during our years of living on Blaine Branch. And one more was at Rabun Gap. After Uncle Jess and Aunt Lazelle moved into their new home on Vinson Road, while I was there one day, my aunt asked me to dispose of a broken churn. Now a churn was a large pottery crock with a wooden dasher which was used to make butter from milk. While carrying it in my hands, a large piece fell, gashing open my right hand in two places.

Another time, while visiting the site of a church which was being built a few miles from our home, I was walking on the open floor joists and slipped, plunging to the foundation, and striking my chin on a cinder block.

"I love watching the birds, Mama. We got something in the mail about a society for birds. Audubon. They send out books and stickers and stuff. Can I send off for it?"

"That's a good organization. You're making your own money now caddying. If you want to join the

National Audubon Society and pay for it yourself, I think that would be nice."

"Great. I'll send it off today! I've already got it ready."

My mother pursed her lips and I saw the corners turn up ever so slightly. "Do you know how to catch a bird?" she asked.

"How?"

"You sneak up on it and put salt on its tail."

"Oh, Mama! You're so funny!" I laughed so hard I nearly choked.

Before I got my own bicycle, I had a trike and a wagon. But I clearly needed something better. One day, while walking home from caddying at Franklin, I found a beautiful bicycle just lying by the road. I looked around and called for whoever may have owned it—but no one was to be found. I wanted a bike so badly that I jumped on it and soon I was riding! I rode that wonderful bicycle all the way home.

"Where did you get that bicycle, Stanley?" I knew that foreboding tone in my mother's voice.

"It was just setting beside the road. I tried to find the owner."

"Son, now you know better than to take something that doesn't belong to you! You take it right back where you got it this minute!"

Sheepishly, I bowed my head and obeyed. Of *course* I knew better! When I reached the turn in the road in which I had found it, I saw a young boy, glad to see his ride returning.

Soon, I bought myself a bike. Never again was I tempted to take anything that wasn't mine. My parents made sure I remembered my indiscretion. They believed in the Biblical principle, "spare the rod and spoil the child".

On my twelfth birthday, August 17th, 1958, my parents gifted me with a brand new Daisy BB gun. Finally I was ready to at least do a little hunting on my own.

"Be careful with that thing, Stanley," my mother said.

"Don't worry," I told her. "I'll be careful."

Soon a bright male cardinal lit in the walnut tree by the meadow fence to the west of the cabin. I set my sight and squeezed the trigger. I really don't believe I thought I would really hit it. But, alas, when that striking bird failed to fly, I knew I had done the unthinkable. Then, drips of crimson blood descended toward the turf below and my heart sank. Tears flooded my big brown eyes. His claws retained a death grip on the limb.

I dashed into the house and informed my frowning mother of my deed. I was made to climb the tree and release the dear bird. I thought about all the beautiful pictures I had gotten from the Audubon Society. *You sneak up on it and put salt on its tail.* I ran into the pantry, scrambled up the ladder to my bed and buried my head in my pillow. I had killed the North Carolina state bird. My gun and I were both grounded.

Early that year I had become more aware of a need for spiritual help and training. My mother, teacher she was, was adamant in her feeling that I needed this guidance and relationship with God. I was obedient and wanted to be all that I should be. I knelt by my bed, asked God for guidance and confessed my faith in Christ. We had been attending non-denominational services at a little storefront mission in Franklin. From this work a weekly radio ministry began which I often attended. Later I was baptized.

My uncle, Dan, had felt a call and need for a perm- anent chapel and campground, and constructed a building for the beginning of such a ministry on his farm in the Mulberry Community, near the North

Carolina–Georgia line. My father sometimes also exhorted at services. We would go each Sunday morning, often continuing to the radio station in Franklin. It was during this revival atmosphere that I began feeling a personal call to Christian service and ministry.

Also that winter, our excellent hunter, Rover, who had treed everything from 'possums to muskrats and squirrels went one better. He dug up the most precious stripped baby skunk. He actually looked a bit like him. No mother could be found. We boys wouldn't rest until my parents agreed to let us keep it. My tomboy mother, who would even catch blacksnakes and show them off, could hardly say "get that wild animal out of here!"

We named him Scampy and he became the most loveable pet we would ever have in our care. He was friendly with our cats (we now had five) and our dogs. He was released into the wild every night, and was always back at our door at exactly 6:00 o'clock each morning, incessantly scratching—as if he had an inner alarm clock. His sense of time was truly spooky. It seemed he was awaking us to apprize us of the fact that it was breakfast time—his breakfast time.

Then, in the fall, an occasional dawn would slip by without his timely call. When more frequently than not our friend was absent, we were confident that the instinctive call of nature had whisked him away. As in the movie, *Bambi,* he was surely "twitterpated".

Later we were informed that a neighbor had emptied his shotgun into a skunk which had suddenly appeared on his porch. We were very saddened.

Gary with his Broman guitar

Chapter Eight

Our faithful dog, Rover, now had a mate—Dixie. She was a classy little white Shepherd-mix with black spots which appeared to have been randomly thrown onto her sleek, furry body. She just seemed perfect for our Rover. That fall, the blissful couple gave birth to a litter of four darling young ones.

"Oh, Mama! Can we keep them?" I asked.

"Certainly not! We already have two dogs! We will find good homes for them."

"Oh, please! How about just one of 'em? Just look at those eyes! And he's a boy!"

"Oh, alright," Mama huffed. Just him, the others have to go! What are you going to name him?"

"Well, I said, he looks a lot like Scampy—and he's not coming back. I want to name him after Scampy!"

"Sounds good, Mike said, smiling broadly.

Anthony, who had been staying with Uncle Steve, where Lonnie had also previously lived, was with us by this time, and the colorful shades of autumn were fading to a neutral winter brown. We had previously explored the surrounding hills and discovered a tiny opening which disappeared into a hillside on a tree farm nearby. We knew that we would not likely get permission to explore this mysterious cave, so we all went to the house and obtained some paper bags, an old broom handle, a wire, some candles and a box of matches. Gary the Great insisted on carrying the "torch" — the broomstick tightly wrapped in torn paper bags on the end, attached with the wire and doused with dripping candle wax, lit with a match. We considered this venture a secret plub mission. This decision made any venture officially the right thing to do.

Once we had entered, it was obvious that we were in an old abandoned mine. Deep from within the creeks of faltering timbers screamed their objections in no uncertain terms.

"Let's get out of here!" I said anxiously.

As we eased outward, I breathed a deep sigh, thinking all danger was past.

On the bank, Gary started dabbing the dead grasses with the torch.

"What are you doing?" Mike yipped. "You'll start something you can't put out!"

"Have no fear, Gary's here!" His lip curled.

Suddenly a puff of harsh fall breeze caught the flames, and carried it to other grasses and brush. Frantically, all of us began fighting the fire with our coats, and stomping around us. "I'll go for help," Anthony said frantically.

Volunteers were called from not only our county, but all of the surrounding ones. But the flames flew onward, devouring a distant neighbor's "Honor Farm" of tender pines.

The local newspaper, the Franklin Press, carried the broad headline, "Tom Sawyers Burn 100 Acres of Prize Trees."

"See," said Gary, his lips pursing in a deliberate simper, "I'm Tom Sawyer. The paper said so!"

Marvin and Allen in front of the cabin

on Blaine Branch

Chapter Nine

That November 30th old Mrs. Laura Jones, General's mother, quietly passed away. [2] Rather than leave her body in the funeral home, the family held an all-night wake at their house, a rather common practice in those days. The entire neighborhood turned out, even us kids. It seemed that we were packed into that somber atmosphere like so many clothes pins threatening to fall from a line. As the stillness of night faded to morning, somewhere in those wee hours, the sand filled my eyes and I drifted off. I awoke as my dad huddled me lovingly in his massive arms and laid me in my mother's lap in our old green truck.

During the time my cousins were with us at the little cabin on Blaine Branch, two of my father's brothers from Virginia brought their families to visit. Uncle Allen came with his children. The oldest was Allen II, whom we called Junior. Next came tall Barbara, who reminded me of her mother, Aunt Geneva; then Roger, Wanda and Brenda, respectively. The kids ranged in age from fifteen down to about ten. Their visit was pleasurable, and Uncle Allen, who had a jolly nature and sense of humor, got a real kick out of playing with our boisterous goats.

Next came Uncle Johnny, Daddy's only older sibling. He and his wife, Toy, had only two young daughters, Patty and Betty. They arrived in the winter of 1958-1959. Gary and I were in our seventh school year. Gary immediately became attracted to Betty's silky blonde hair and alluring smile. At almost thirteen, he was going through that first stage of growing into male-hood. Since it was winter, we mostly stayed inside, hovering around the crackling fire. But the visit was enriching, and I was delighted that they had cared enough to come.

Four of my mother's brothers had chosen barbering as their life's profession, and Dan and Steve jointly operated the Palmer Street Barber Shop on the steep hill going in toward the heart of Franklin. Being a tight-knit and generous family, I was never charged for haircuts. A fact that I later realized I could have insisted that they do. I could have paid something.

"Let's go hunting," Mike said to me one autumn Saturday afternoon.

"Sure," I responded, "We don't have anything else to do."

When we left we were always accompanied by at least Rover. This time he, alone, followed. After about forty-five minutes we had climbed to a distant mountaintop on the eastern horizon. I believe we were on the Jones place. Back then neighbors didn't care much about things like trespassing. Grey chestnut trunks, dead fifty years from the blight, and giant sleeping oaks filled our path. There we followed the spine of the ridge, giving no heed to the boundaries we were crossing, but eyeing occasional markers to facilitate our homeward journey. Suddenly, our faithful companion sniffed his way to a narrow opening in the leaf-covered floor. His shrill voice announced a presence beneath the crusty surface. Fervently, he pawed his way toward the object of his pressing endeavor. After much ado he arrived at the bed of a dormant, but much-alive, groundhog.

Breaking a forked bough from a fallen tree, I carefully pinned the once-drowsy creature's head to the ground while Mike grasped his dark, furry stub of a tail. Our catch was squirming viciously, making every effort to leave a lasting impression on the hand of his captor.

"We'll never be able to bring him home like this," Mike said with a frown. "You go to the house and get a tow sack and I'll stay here and hold him down till you get back."

To my eager cousin, it seemed an eternity before my return. I was notably exhausted from scurrying up hills and trudging through drifts of crunchy dead leaves. Mile's muscles were taut and sore from wrestling with the unpredictable notions of our proud prisoner.

A curtain of darkness was descending rapidly. When we finally arrived safely at home with our uninvited guest, my parents were not nearly as pleased as we. We were only allowed to keep him briefly before returning him to the wild.

That winter we ran out of corn for our chickens, hogs and cattle. My dad was now plowing with a small red Farmall tractor. He had sold Jane and Jocko had died in the worst of times. He had been forced to carve out a deep grave on a frozen hillside with a mattock and shovel — a grueling task which took several days, even with what little help us boys could muster.

The summer's crop had been very scant. Corn was, of course, more scarce and expensive. After much ado, my dad finally found a farmer who had offered to allow us to salvage the leftover corn from his snow and ice-covered field. A locale which reminded me of the pictures I had seen of the Alaskan tundra. What was worse, we were to haul our gleanings to his house and give him half of it! Even at my young age this arrangement seemed ludicrous. All of us boys, Daddy, and Uncle Rowe plunged our fingers into that mass of ice and dug out those scattered nubbins until our hands were numb. But my father never complained. We salvaged enough grain to suffice until we could buy more.

Blaine Branch was not only a peaceful rambling stream which served to define our happy little hollow, but it was a source of many hours of searching for precious stones—rubies and garnets. My mother owned a set of World Book Encyclopedias which I have retained to this day. She had purchased them in Wyoming during her first school term at Springwillow School near Sheridan in 1930.

"Look here," I said one day while searching in the volume with the article on Rubies. "This says that Macon County North Carolina is the only place in the Western Hemisphere where true rubies are found!" I could hardly believe my eyes. I collected a number of miniscule rubies as well as some impressive garnets. I also discovered that the hills held many quartz and even turquoise pieces. The hobby of collecting became a passion for me which led to a significant number of varied collections. But I had come about this collecting passion honestly. Mama had accumulated books since childhood. They had been the only items which her father had allowed aboard their loaded truck when leaving Wyoming for the move back south. A great number of these tomes remain a part of my library to this day.

Gary and I both loved sketching caricatures and futuristic cars. One of us made up a cartoon character named Mr. Huck-gug-oyee-oyee. Both of us claimed him, so I dare not be adamant about this. Everything Gary did, I thought I had to try to do…but I never did them better. Gary learned to play guitar quite well, and was given Uncle Dan's vintage Broman. I solicited his help in learning, and did a fair job at it. We both started writing songs at an early age. And poetry became of great import to me.

Gary's first effort was catchy, and I listened intently as the melodious words came forth and the Broman played along.

" ♫ I can tell a story about an Alaskan guy, who made a mistake and now must die—yes him and his family, too. If you go there, don't let it happen to you! ♫"

Even as we grew toward adolescence, as long as my cousins were around, the plub continued to live. In warm months, when we were all doing our chores at the barn, we would conduct our business in that old corncrib, and have corncob fights using bushel-basket lids tied to our arms with baling wire as shields. Other times we would arm wrestle to improve our preparedness for our imagined battle with our impending invaders.

Nelson and Rhonda were the only ones who never spent any time with us at the cabin. Nelson spent some time with Uncle Jess, and Rhonda was almost adopted by a couple at Mountain City, Georgia named Peggy and Tony Lawson. They ran the post office and general store there, and had a delightful assortment of creatures at home. These included a playful monkey and a talking Mina bird coincidentally named "Mike".

During the summer of 1959, my cousins all went away. First Mike expended some months with Uncle Dan. Then he and Gary went to boarding school at Tallulah Falls and Tamassee DAR in North Georgia. I was lost. I was once again an only child. I returned to caddying at Franklin. Another way I made money was by finding and selling golf balls which had been lost and left in the "rough".

One day that summer, while on the fifth fairway, a golfer hit a ball which struck me directly in the belt buckle. Thank God for that large belt buckle. The wind was knocked out of my slender, limp body, but I was soon on my feet, denying my need for a doctor.

Mike with two of our goats, summer 1960

Chapter Ten

The next school year, all was like a different world. Not only did the house seem empty, the Macon County School System was now in reorganization. I was bused to Union Elementary for my eighth grade year. And the fabulous and prestigious plub was over. By this time Mary Hopkins had a new name — Bingham. She had been adopted by her grandparents. It seemed that she was taking on a brighter personality. She became a good friend and we were able to converse about the new school and the constant changes in our valley. My teacher there was also the school principal. His name was Harry Moses, and along with the seventh grade teacher, Curtis Owens, he also ran a successful real estate agency. Mr. Moses noticed my sketching on my papers and came down on me for altering a portrait of George Washington to look more like George Jones. But he liked me. And he let me go out for basketball and play on second string. I made every game, and truly enjoyed it. But he could tell that art was more of a passion for me. Moses and Owens had designed a mountain-top amusement park which was to be constructed between Franklin and Sylva, in Macon County near its border with neighboring Jackson County. Mr. Moses asked me to make the first drawing of what they envisioned for this nature-based venture. This forty-acre park was, and still is, named "Gold City". There, visitors may mine for precious stones such as rubies, amethysts, sapphires and emeralds. Macon County is now known as the "Gem Capitol of the World".

Not only was I privileged to draw the initial layout for Gold City, but also the plan for the Moses' new home. The park has long been under new management, but my friends at Union School were the designers, with a tiny bit of my help at age thirteen.

That September, as the Macon County Fair was about to get underway, a large snapping turtle was creeping across the road near our house. Finding a stick with which to hold down his leathery head, I captured the big fellow, and placed him carefully in a washtub.

"Mama, they're giving a prize for the ugliest pet at the fair, and I'm gonna enter this turtle."

My mother frowned, and then smiled. "Okay, you may have something there."

I guess when I saw the competition I knew I would end up the winner of the blue ribbon. The fair would also serve as a showplace for some of my artwork which would do well in its class.

On Tuesday, February 3rd, while listening to my transistor radio on the way home from Union Elementary School, the news that met my ears was overwhelming.

"We interrupt this broadcast to bring you the following bulletin: we now have the details on earlier reports concerning the suspected crash of the small Beechcraft plane which was carrying rock-and-roll musicians Buddy Holly, Richie Valens, and J. P. Richardson, known as the "Big Bopper", to a concert. The wreckage of the plane has been found near Clear Lake, Iowa. The small private plane, which took off at 12:55 central time this morning, was spotted shortly thereafter by the plane's owner, who stated that he 'saw the taillight of the aircraft gradually descend until it was out of sight'. A flight plan was filed a couple of hours later and a search ensued. Sometime before 10:00 AM the plane was spotted. It has now been confirmed that there were no survivors.

"Buddy Holly has already been a great influence on popular music with such songs as 'Peggy Sue', 'That'll Be the Day', and 'Maybe Baby'. Richie Valens is best known for his smash hit 'Donna', while the Big Bopper's best selling record has been his rendition of 'Chantilly Lace'. The popular music industry has taken a great loss today."

I bowed my head and said a prayer for their families as tears formed in my eyes.

Later the tragic death of these singers was immortalized as "the day the music died" by Don McLean in his lengthy classic ballad "American Pie". [9]

Sometimes, after my cousins left. I would go up the hill on autumn weekends and play with the younger Jones children. I enjoyed watching the *Three Stooges* and *Our Gang* with them, and on Saturday nights, after our TV went on the blink, I would go and watch *Bonanza* with Frankie and Nancy quite often.

My term in eighth grade marked my first genuine interest in the opposite sex. But I was too shy to exhibit my emotions, though I did daydream about them—especially one of them—a lovely brunette cheerleader. Perhaps she was another reason to make every game.

One of the most unforgettable highlights of that year was our eighth grade trip to Atlanta. The trip itself was really no big deal to me because I had been there more than once before, and had lived for three years in the city of Canton, Ohio. We stayed at the famous Henry Grady Hotel. My roommate had evidently never been out of the county in which he was born. All of a sudden, as I was just getting sound asleep, he was wide awake, shaking me and telling me that it was daylight, thus, time to rise and shine.

"I don't think so, man," I grunted. "I just went to sleep. Turn on the radio."

He did, and almost the first words out of the announcer's mouth proved my point. "Time, 12:00 o'clock midnight."

"Get your clothes off and get back in the bed!" I yelled.

Another memorable event during my eighth grade trip was visiting the state capitol and meeting then governor, Ernest Vandiver. Later I was to see him again — closer to home.

After most of the next summer had passed at the golf course, Uncle Atlas, my mother's then unmarried brother who now made his home in Atlanta, asked permission to take me for the following school year. I could be like the son he would never have. He came one weekend and whisked me away to "civilization". At that time he worked at a barber shop near Buckhead, in a prosperous section of the city. Of course, once again, there was no need to pay for haircuts. Even when I couldn't make it to one of my uncles while growing up, my mother did the honors.

Talk about a new world! My life was again transformed in an even more drastic measure. Not only did we have running water and a great television, there were all sorts of modern conveniences all around me. On Saturday nights my loving uncle would take me downtown, often to the Varsity Drive Inn near Georgia Tech where we would order our evening meal and watch color television. Of course not all of the shows were in color. *The Rebel, Have Gun, Will Travel* and the *Rifleman* weren't—but *Bonanza* was. My favorite! Then we would usually go to a theater (the fabulous Fox was the rage in those days) and see a war flick, then look at new cars and grab a Sunday morning paper before heading home! Those were the days for a fourteen-year-old from the country.

The school I attended was brand new Cross Keys High. I loved Spanish class where my teacher was dubbed "Chico" and we did whatever it took to get kicked out of class. Things like throwing spitballs and shifting seats to confuse the little guy. Then I was also in the Spanish Club. I don't know how I made it through that year.

Another novelty was having a classmate in English class named Bill who had transferred in from Texas where he had been in Dan Blocker's English class before he began acting. He, of course, was now "Hoss" on my *Bonanza*. My first English teacher, Miss Trapp, resigned to get married, and was replaced by Miss Butler. She was very supportive of my poetical interest, and recognized me as an "aspiring poet". I don't know if she really believed that, or was just being nice to me.

While I was in Atlanta I missed working, so I checked the paper for jobs. I had already sold mottos, greeting cards and golf balls. Surely I could sell anything, so with my kind uncle's permission, I accepted a position going door-to-door showing fabric samples and selling furniture upholstery jobs. For this task the store owner assigned me to a low-income area where he felt that his services might be needed.

I caught the city bus to the area one Saturday morning. I got an order right away which was pending. I felt on top of the world—until I knocked on a door and a lady answered without a stitch of clothing on. I went back and turned in my kit immediately. Maybe door-to-door in Atlanta wasn't my cup of tea at that age.

I know I must have worried my dear uncle to the limit, though it was nothing compared with what goes on today with drugs and wild parties. One day, out of the clear blue, I decided I was going to turn my black hair blond. Shows what I knew. I used regular dye, and my hair became a sickening orange.

Another, even more harrowing experience, occurred one winter Saturday evening when I boarded a city bus to travel across town to Lakewood Park to a tent revival meeting. I stayed till about 11:30 and caught the first available bus downtown to Five Points where I was to transfer from the Lakewood bus to the 23 Oglethorpe back to Brookhaven, where we called home. Upon arriving, I was shocked to learn that the transit system halted all routes at midnight and didn't resume service until 6:00 AM. Of course there was no such animal as a cell phone, and I was flat broke. I didn't even have the dime it took then for a pay phone. Here I was, fourteen years of age, in the heart of downtown Atlanta, stuck on the street all night long. Today I would likely be killed.

Despondent, but somehow calm, I paced the street, eventually coming to rest over a warm-air vent on the sidewalk. My poor uncle must have had a near-sleepless night before I finally showed up that Sunday morning around 7:00.

Steve and family, December, 1960

Chapter Eleven

It seemed that my freshman year in Atlanta had expired far too rapidly, leaving within my heart a distant dream of escaping to the city for good when high school was history.

I was glad to be with my parents, but the little cabin on Blaine Branch seemed too tiny to encase my dreams of a prosperous future where my ambitions could reach fruition. And I had grown quite fond of my uncle who cared enough to show me what life could be like in the real world. The rural lifestyle had sheltered me to the realities which slapped me in the face in the big city. But this had been fortunate. And the next three years in the cabin would be endearing and later prove invaluable to my life experience.

The summer of my return I discovered that my "bro-cuzes" were back from boarding school and home with their father. They were now traveling up the curvy mountain road each day to caddy at Highlands Country Club. Now this was the big time! I had found hitch-hiking a simple method to get to where I needed to be, so each morn, off I went, riding my thumb to Highlands. Here I could make more money and meet some outstanding folks. Georgia Governor

Ernest Vandiver was a regular there, and his caddy became a personal friend of mine.

One Sunday afternoon, while visiting with Uncle Rowe and his boys at Rabun Gap, Gary was excited about his recent accomplishments.

"Rockets?" I said, "How do you make rockets?"

"See, I take a sheet of tinfoil and roll some of it around a pencil. Then I twist up one end and make a nose for my rocket. Then I take some of these shotgun shells and empty out the gunpowder and pour it in, like so." He was demonstrating his fascinating "invention" as he went. "Then I use the pencil to pack it and make a wick. Come on, I'll show you."

I anxiously followed, my mind whirling. Setting the rocket beside a rock launching pad, he lit the small wick and we watched it zoom into the heavens.

Why did Gary always come up with the good stuff?

The next school year, at age fifteen, I was able to take Driver's Training. I had a great instructor, Frank Ramsey. Looking back, that year seems to have been somewhat uneventful. I had Mrs. Martin for Biology, Mrs. Waldroop for General Science, Mr. Crawford for

Algebra, and Mrs. Standley for Spanish. Oh, yes, I took more Spanish and joined the Spanish Club again. Now *el mundo fue mio*!

I do know that my sophomore year went well, and I was able to reconnect with my old classmates whom I had originally met, both in Mrs. Meadows' third grade class and Mr. Moses' eighth grade class, and make some new friends.

The following summer I saved my caddying money, and not only paid for my clothes and personal needs, I was out shopping for a car.

I saw an ad in the Franklin Press that caught my eye—a powerful pale green 1953 V-8 Mercury.

When I showed up, the lady owner was overly reluctant.

"I don't think this is the right car for a teenage boy! I'm afraid you'd wreck and maybe kill yourself in it."

"But I'd be careful," I said, "I wouldn't be driving that fast. I'm working and I need it to get back and forth to Highlands."

"Highlands! Around those curvy roads? I don't think so. I'd never forgive myself if you got hurt."

So my dream of the Mercury was dashed. I went to a local car lot and made a less-fanciful deal. On my sixteenth birthday I paid cash for a 1950 Chevy — $100.00. I got my driver's license the same day as my car. Now I could get out on my own and explore the exciting world. And for the rest of the summer I could drive to Highlands to work. Gas was an average of .299 per gallon. And when gas wars came, it would get down to less than twenty cents.

But during that summer that I bought my first car, I met another boy, just older than myself, who had become a close friend. His name was Clyde Wilson, and he lived in another hollow in the Patton Valley on Dobson Road. He had two sisters named Betty and Mamie who would sometimes visit with him.

When the fair came I had only had my Chevy for a short while. After the fair closed that Saturday night, Clyde and I decided to take a short ride to the neighboring town of Bryson City and "find out what was happening".

It turned out that Bryson City was just like Franklin at midnight — dead. And before the night was over I would almost wish I were.

After I had parked and we had strolled up and down the empty main drag, we returned to my limousine and started home. The street lights shone brightly, and as the two of us shot the breeze, I heard a siren behind us.

"Please step out of the car. I need to see your driver's license and registration."

"Certainly, officer," I said in surprise. "What did I do wrong?"

"You were driving with no headlights on. Would you please get back in your car and turn on your lights so I can see if everything works right."

"Oh, certainly, sir. I'm sure sorry! We were just talking, and the lights were so bright out there that I just forgot to turn them on."

"What are you two young men doing in Bryson City this time of night, anyway? You're a little far from home, aren't you?"

"Yes, sir," I said. "We were at the Macon County fair tonight and just wanted to ride around and talk."

"Well, you'll need to come back next month for court and tell your little story to the judge," the officer said, handing me a citation.

"Can I just pay this ticket," I asked.

"If you'd rather, come to the police department here on Monday. The address is on there. It will cost you sixty dollars."

My heart sank. I could hear my mother. It would not be a pretty picture when I got home.

Betty and Mamie Wilson in our yard

Wiley Jones house and barn in background

Chapter Twelve

I was certainly right. My parents were both up and waiting for me when I arrived home at about 1:00 that chilly Sunday morning. I was hopelessly grounded. It was just days before the beginning of my junior year, and I was made to drive back to Bryson City on Monday morning and face the somber music alone. I had to pay the entire fine with my own money. I could not drive anywhere but to work, and I was given an early curfew to be home each evening. I was to set up weekly payments, then drive to Bryson City each week and take them in person, and further humiliate myself. I must also bring the receipts home for proof that I had done so. If I could act like a child, I could prove that I was behaving responsibly. I also could not visit with my friend, Clyde Wilson.

Early in my junior year I traded my car for another one almost identical to it, but two-toned. Both cars were brown, but the old one was a solid light color and the new one had a rich, chocolate-colored top. That year I was able to drive both to school, on occasions, and to Spanish Club meetings. Though I was never involved in athletics in high school, I still loved basketball, and made it to a number of home games. I was proud to be a Panther.

And that year I was blessed to come to know a most delightful lady who showed me great favor. Her mother had been my fifth grade teacher. Her name was Jean Hemphill. She was to be my Arts and Crafts teacher for the two final years at Franklin High. She taught me the remarkable art of silk screen printing and sent one of my prints to New York for national competition.

She and her dear mother hired me to work at their home and do gardening for them. I truly relished their company and I knew that they both appreciated me. I had many teachers that I liked and enjoyed, but Miss Hemphill will always hold a special place in my heart and mind. We shall return to her later.

I decided one Friday night during my junior year while still driving my two-toned '50 Chevy to go to the drive-in theatre alone to catch a movie. The speaker next to my door was out of order, so I went to the other side where there was no one parked and pulled the wire across and hung it in my front passenger window. *There's more than one way to skin a cat, where there's a will there's a way.* My mother's old sayings rang in my ears. Mission accomplished! *All's well that ends well.* That was another of my dear mother's favorite platitudes.

As soon as the words "THE END" flashed upon the gigantic silver screen, I pulled off—the speaker still securely attached to my window. Other cars were joining me in exiting. I was so embarrassed that I didn't know what to do. I surely realized that I shouldn't keep driving, but I did anyway. As soon as I was comfortably out of the lot and at a stopping place, I pulled over and placed the speaker inside the car.

As I cruised home I worked out my plan. I would drive back the next day and tell the theater owner what I had done and that it had certainly been un-intentional.

When I walked through our front room door, my mother was sitting there, looking up at me. Immediately I made a complete confession of what had happened. With my mother, I knew it was useless to try to get away with anything anyway.

Early the next morning, before I had been able to drive back to town, a sheriff car pulled into our drive.

I've had it now, I thought.

"Stanley, the deputy said quietly, the owner of the drive-in theater said that your car was seen leaving there last night with one of their speakers still in your window."

"Yes sir," I swallowed hard. "It was an accident. I didn't realize it till I was pulling out. I was going to take it back today. I'm really sorry."

"Don't worry about it, son," the deputy said, a slight smile coming to his lips as he spoke. "He's not pressing charges. He just wants his speaker back,"

I breathed deep.

"Oh, thank you, sir. Tell him I really appreciate it. I'll get it for you."

"Just watch it next time and make darn sure this doesn't happen again!"

"You can be sure it won't, sir,"

I guess one of my mother's sayings was right in this case—all's well that ends well.

Trula, Atlas, Rowe, "Mom" Ethel and Mike

May 1962

Chapter Thirteen

My good friend, Clyde Wilson, along with his parents and sisters, Mamie and Betty, had moved out of the area. That saddened me, because after my grounding was over, we had been able to renew our times together. I really didn't have close friends in my sophomore and junior years at dear old Franklin High, and I was too shy to date.

Daddy became very ill and finally had to go to bed. He had always seemed basically healthy other than his stomach. Going to a doctor was something we never did while I was growing up. My uncle Rowe came and helped my mother with work while I was away caddying. Finally, after everyone pleaded with him, Daddy gave in and went to see Dr. Ed Angel.

"This is extremely serious," Dr. Angel told my mother. "X-rays show that his appendix has been burst for about two weeks. I don 't see how he has lived this long."

"Well, everyone has prayed for him a lot," Mama told him.

"It's nothing short of a miracle. But he has to have emergency surgery at once."

"Of course, Dr Angel. You know what's best."

The good doctor shook his head and had my father prepped for surgery. The recovery was slow and painful, but my father was a tough and stubborn man. He made a full and hearty recovery. He just worried about his doctor bill and the whopping $400 hospital bill until everything was all paid off.

Ever since the loss of our dear Scampy, I had longed for another pet skunk. We loved our cats and our dogs; Rover, Dixie and Scampy's young namesake, but none of them could fill the void for me that the loss of our skunk had caused.

One Saturday during the spring of my junior year, while out with the dogs, I was thrilled to see a baby skunk come dashing across my path. Quickly, I grabbed it and grasped it close to my chest. I knew that it was so young that its odor bag was not yet developed. Another thing I had learned from the previous experience of caring for Scampy was that when cared for by loving persons they would never use their natural defense mechanism against their caregivers.

What a beautiful specimen she was! With wide white stripes from her head to the very tip of her tail, she reminded me for the world of Flower in the *Bambi* movie. So I named her that.

I knew that for a time we must keep her in the cabin until we were certain that she was fully domesticated and dependent upon us.

Another Saturday, when I had only been Flower's provider for a few weeks, we had gone to Franklin to get our week's supply of groceries in Daddy's old pickup. While my mother was shopping for groceries at the A&P, it dawned on me that she had set a rat trap in the pantry. There had been evidence that we were being infested by a creature that we didn't need, and she was taking the proper steps to rid us of it before the damage grew any greater. But what really was weighing on my mind was the upsetting fact that I had opened the pantry door to get something for my mother, and didn't remember closing it...Flower was in the front room, which included the kitchen and living area. My heart raced until we could return and check to make sure my dear little Flower was safe.

Upon arriving, I bolted in and checked the trap. My worst fears were confirmed. Once again I was without my favorite pet — but this time I blamed myself.

"Mom and Pop" Vinson at Rabun Gap 1962

Chapter Fourteen

"You're not gonna believe this, Darling," Daddy said one day in 1963. "I won the recliner at the furniture store in the drawing!"

Mama smiled. "We've never won anything before. Where would we put it? There's no room anywhere in the house for it."

"Maybe Atlas would want it," Daddy said. "He's taken your parents down to Atlanta now. Maybe he needs a nice chair like that."

"I'll write to him and ask him."

Daddy took the plush crimson Lazy-Boy recliner carefully from the bed of the truck and sat it on the porch. With his taut biceps, hoisting furniture seemed as simple for him as lifting a pillow would have for me. It was wrapped in a heavy clear plastic cover which would protect it from the elements until it could be moved.

Within a week my mother had received an answer. My uncle was definitely interested and would pay them a fair price. After driving up, he was loading the chair and taking it home. My grandmother received many years of comfort from that beautiful recliner.

Daddy's old truck was giving him a lot of problems. He had met a Mr. Ashe who had a red Jeep pickup for sale. He took me with him to go look at it.

"What do you think about that Jeep, Stanley?" Daddy had taken me to the side in Ashe's garage.

"I like it, Daddy. You know red's my favorite color."

"Well, I think I'll make him an offer."

Daddy went back over to where Mr. Ashe was working on another car.

"I like your Jeep pretty well, but it needs a paint job, and I really wanted another Chevy. I'll give you $350 cash for it like it is." He had asked $500.

"You drive a hard bargain, Sinclair. How about $400."

"St. Clair, the name's St. Clair. I'll split the difference and go $375, but that's my final offer, take it or leave it."

"Well, you sure drive a hard bargain, anyway, Marvin. Okay. I'll make you out a bill of sale and get the title and sign it over to you."

One thing I learned from my dad was the principle of bargaining. He would often take pigs or calves to the local stock pen and keep them outside rather than running them through the sale. He would listen to the stock report on the radio, and knew what the going price per pound was that day in major markets. Then he would find buyers outside without having to pay the fee charged to run them through the pen.

My dad was also a skillful master of estimating the weight of livestock. He could take one look at a hog or cow and guess its weight within two to three pounds with startling accuracy. I remember clearly how awe-struck I was by his uncanny ability.

The swine business was our main livelihood for almost all of the time that we lived on the farm on Blaine Branch Road. But in the summer of 1963 the market fluctuated so drastically and so frequently that my father finally felt that this volatile business was no longer profitable. Normally six week old pigs brought ten dollars. With the expense of caring for the brood sows, buying pig starter and grower rations, and marketing them, it was imperative that this average be maintained. Prices dropped to around six dollars per pig at weaning time. This was just not enough to turn a profit; so, in utter frustration, my father sold every porker, from the oldest to the youngest, in our lots and vowed to never look back. From then on he would only rely on cattle. And every time he had a farm after that, he always stuck by his decision.

One **of our goats named Pee Wee**

Chapter Fifteen

I continued to commute back and forth to Highlands for my final summer of caddying in 1963. The music was gradually evolving. The Beatles, the Animals, and the Rolling Stones had swept across America as a flood. The Supremes and other Motown groups were rocking and rolling through the minds of every red-blooded American teen. Bobby Vinton and Bobby Vee also turned us on.

At Highlands a popular hangout for us caddies was Bill's Soda Shop downtown. What a "jive joint" that place was. We could order a malted, a shake, or just our favorite soda.

In the car I could catch the latest songs on the AM hit parades, but I always had my transistor radio with me—by now a much more sophisticated model than the tiny one I owned when I was younger.

I knew all the words by heart and they rambled through my mind every day. " ♫ Roses are red, my love, violets are blue, sugar is sweet, my love, good luck, may God bless you! ♪"

That summer a nasty fight broke out in the caddy lot. One young man came at another with a pocket knife. The caddies involved were suspended and asked to leave immediately. Discipline was strict and I was glad.

The trailer which we had brought from Ohio nine years earlier finally got a family to live in it for a while that year. At church we had met a family which became close to us and needed a place to stay. The lady was a divorced mother with three girls and one son. The middle daughter was a cute freckled red-head, and I became quickly interested in her. But she was considerably younger than I was. Still, she was the closest I had come to having a real girlfriend. Her mother soon moved away and I didn't see her as often, but I did feel deeply for that girl.

Then it was back to school for my final year.

One crisp day that fall I got my 410 shotgun out which I had bought that summer, and with Scampy, headed for the woods. What a sharp little gun it was, with a highly polished knotty-maple stock and a soft plastic carrying case!

Rover was growing very old, and he and Dixie didn't offer to come along that day. I walked through the old hog lot and lingered under the big weeping willow tree before climbing across the slumping hog-wire fence and strolling through the stubble field which remained from harvesting the corn crop. Daddy needed less now that the hogs no longer occupied their crumbling domain. Somehow it seemed lonely without them. A goat brushed my leg and stared up at me, letting out a pitiful bleat. The goats were being allowed to devour the remaining stalks which now had little other usefulness. As I ambled onward, the memories of my childhood glory days flooded my mind. For the first time in years I recalled that day so many years ago when I wandered far away and discovered the mystifying field with the thistles and the rambling rock wall. Why had this been blocked from my memory for all of these years? I must have gone near there while out with my cousins. *Come to think of it, we usually hunted on the other side of the road, up past the site of Vinsonville, I reasoned. Just when we found the cave and the forest fire started, were we over this way, and then we turned right and went more north!*

It had been too long. I couldn't remember the way I had gone to that wondrous spot, but I knew that now that I had thought of it, I would somehow find it once again. A crow let out a startled caw and flew rapidly from a white pine to my right. *Something looks strangely familiar about that pine!* I shook my head. *A white pine is a white pine, right? Wait!* The trunk forked about half way up, forming two distinct new equal trunks! Yes! It seemed that the crow was speaking to me, "Caw! Remember this tree?" I thought of Poe's prolific classic poem, "The Raven" producing in my mind a nostalgic sense of wonder, and on my arms, a startling cascade of chill bumps. At that point it seemed that I was guided by an inner power, leading me onward toward my goal. New markers appeared. Within fifteen short minutes the sun again revealed the opening I had seen as a child! Déjà vu! There was the site of the mystical thistle patch. No blossoms were present, of course, since the season of their dwelling was half a year away. The old rock wall seemed somehow not as prodigious as it did the last time I had stood in this spot. Nonetheless, I knew that I had found it!

For a few brief moments I merely stood there, as if hypnotized by the renewal of a feeling so long missing in my life. What was it about this spot that intrigued me as it did? Was it the fact that it had loomed so beautifully before me at a special time in my life, or the idea that it had been forbidden? Then, slowly I strolled around the wall and noticed a dull bit of metal burrowed beneath the soil. Reaching down, I scratched it loose and saw that it was an Indian-head penny dated 1898! *Could it have been dropped by the Shopes as they crossed the mountain on their wedding night?* Pushing anxiously forward, I picked up a distinctive arrowhead. Scampy was sniffing the ground in zigzags. Suddenly he plunged forward and began a shrill yipping. I dashed on, trying my best to keep up. Soon I spotted a playful squirrel dashing up a chestnut oak tree. We were at the edge of the great mountain my father had spoken about that day so long ago. I took my eyes from the tree and there, in the side of the mountain, a gurgling stream was flowing out of a cave. The opening was large, so I carefully crept forward, into its gaping mouth. A flashlight was a necessity now when away, and I pulled mine from its case on my side. There, inside that mountain sat a strange contraption. A large rusty metal barrel with copper pipes seemingly growing out. It had been abandoned by its owner for some undeterminable years. I was certain that what I had discovered was the remains of a moonshine still. Now I understood why my father hadn't wanted me to go back there. This forbidden contraption which lay beyond the thistle patch represented to him the vices of the world from which he would have liked for me to remain sheltered. I backed slowly out and gazed upward at Scampy's prize squirrel. Hunting was no longer on my mind.

Stan, 12th grade, fall 1963

Chapter Sixteen

When Clyde Wilson and his family moved away I had no idea that I would ever see them again. But that fall, after I had begun my senior year, one Saturday I was very pleasantly surprised. A late-model Ford pulled up in our driveway and a neatly-dressed young man emerged. I looked at him and wondered what he wanted. As he approached I could tell that he was somehow familiar.

"Hey, Stanley, how are you getting along? Don't you remember me? Clyde Wilson?"

"My goodness. I didn't recognize you! It's great to see you again!"

"I'd like to introduce you to my wife!"

"You're married? Wow! Good to meet you. Won't you come in?"

"Na, we don't have time. We just wanted to come by and see you for a few minutes. I graduated last year and we got married. We're living in Denton."

"Thanks a lot for coming by. This is my last year here, too. I'm planning on moving to Atlanta when I get out of high school. I want to be a commercial artist, so I guess I'll be going to college down there. Don't know where yet."

"Your folks alright?"

"Yeah, they're fine, yours? How about Mamie and Betty?"

"All of us are doing well. My wife and I hope to start a family of our own soon."

I raised my eyebrows. That was something I was trying not to consider. Marriage or a family. But I still missed the red-headed girl.

"Come see us."

"I don't know when I'll be that way. I've never been to Denton."

And that was the last time I ever saw him. But that year I made some really good friends.

Our bus went to Union Elementary to deliver the younger students before taking us on to the high school. At this time I had chosen to ride the bus rather than drive to conserve money. And I was glad I did, because I met a boy named John who would become my new best friend. He had actually transferred in during my junior year. His father was a carpenter, and he was to build for me a bookcase which I had designed which remains with me to this day.

On the bus we would play chess. He taught me the basics, at least enough to beat me every time. A boy called Billy would also join us in the playing of this noble game of skill. But Billy knew how to play well and had a chance against the likes of King John. John and I became such friends as to expend many hours together outside school. I would go to his home and converse at length with his parents while eating many scrumptious home-cooked meals there. We decided to start our own pretend manufacturing business. I wanted to call it HAMCO for Home Arts Manu-facturing Company. He liked the initials, but held a more mischievous name for the acronym to stand for. We created a hard-bodied electric guitar from a 2X12 pine plank as our first and only HAMCO production. But after installing a Radio Shack pick-up it served the purpose well and played lovely music. Well, at least as lovely as my limited talent could muster.

Together we had loads of clean fun. I was even hired by his father as a carpenter's helper and worked on a house which he was building near Wayah Bald.

John's uncle, George, also moved up from Florida and pioneered the first Lutheran church in Macon County.

That year I took mechanical drawing—drafting, as well as my final course in arts and crafts under Miss Jean Hemphill.

"You're so good, but so messy," Miss Hemphill said one day while I was working on a silk screen design.

"Thank you—I think," I said.

"I want you to do the handbook covers for all of the schools in our district this year," she said.

"Now I know I should thank you."

"Start with Franklin Elementary. Then, of course, there's Union and Cowee and Cullasaga and Cartoogechaye...and our school." Jean Hemphill smiled that sweet, simple smile which showed her approval.

Not only did I design these, but also our graduation and baccalaureate covers. I felt so very honored.

The day finally came to vote for senior superlatives. I was chosen the most talented boy and a girl named Alice who played piano exceptionally well won for the girls. I also was granted the art award on college day. I believe that my talent was, and is to a large degree, inspiration. The inspiration given me by my caring parents and teachers like Jean Hemphill.

Kennedy motorcade in Dallas, November 22, 1963

Moments before his assasination

(Photo public domain)[10]

Chapter Seventeen

It was 1:55 PM Eastern Standard Time on Friday, November 22nd, 1963. I had just left Mr. Dick Stott's fifth period Civics class and was in the hall on my way to sixth period English with Mr. Dillard Morrow.

"Did you hear the news?" one of my classmates asked, "Somebody shot President Kennedy!"

"Don't joke about such things," I snapped.

"No, it's for real."

Suddenly a somber voice was blasting from the PA speaker. "About 25 minutes ago, at 12:30 Central Standard Time, as President Kennedy's motorcade was entering Dealy Plaza in downtown Dallas, shots rang out...possibly as many as three. The president was hit in the head. The First Lady, by his side, was unharmed. Texas Governor, John Connally, however, was also shot. Details are sketchy at this time, but I have been told that the president has been rushed to Parkland Hospital. More details as they become available." [9]

I let out a startled gasp. *Surely not in America! What is happening to our country?*

The rest of that horrific day not much was discussed in Franklin High except this horrid tragedy. About an hour later, immediately before the final bell, the dreaded announcement was made. The most beloved president in many years was dead. America was shocked beyond belief.

During my senior year our family started attending a newly-established church in Franklin. In Sunday School class, the teacher became aware of my biblical knowledge and asked me to fill in for her when she became ill. The teens in the class enjoyed my teaching so much that when the regular teacher was well enough to begin teaching again, the class members asked if I could continue to be their teacher. I was pleased at their confidence, yet embarassed. I told the lady that I would gladly step aside and allow her to resume her duties. Because it was the desire of the students, however, I was granted the position of full-time teacher at age seventeen. Some of the class members were even older than I. Thus began my lifelong teaching service.

That year I felt that I was able to step up again. I wanted a newer car, and I had saved my money. One of the DJs at WFSC named Jim had advertised that he wanted to sell his car, a two-tone blue 1955 Chevrolet

Bel-Aire! Man, what a car. It had all the class I wanted.

"Can I test drive it?"

"No," he said, "I don't let anyone drive my car, but I'll take you for a ride in it."

"Okay. Let's go."

"You wantta see the motor?"

"Yeah."

"It's got a 252 six cylinder with a chrome carb cover. It won't go 100 but it'll get you where you want to go and it's easy on gas." Jim shut the hood and told me to get in.

"Well, whatdaya think of my little Chevy?"

"I like it."

"I'm asking $550 cash."

"All I got's $500. That's all I can do. But I'll take good care of it. You saw my '50. I just want something a little newer."

"You seem like a nice kid. I'll take it."

I loved that car, and sometimes wish I still had it today.

When time came for our prom, I was on the decoration committee. We decked the gym out to the hilt. The class hired a band that could get down and nail all our favorite songs.

I had a crush on a girl and asked her be accompany me, but I was too late, she already had a date. I went alone. Something I wouldn't have done even a short time later. But I still enjoyed the music and the company of my classmates.

During that year a lady named Mrs. Snodgrass came to our house with the first home movie camera I had ever seen.

"I love your cabin here. Would you folks mind if I filmed you and your house?"

"That would be fine," Mama said, grinning. "I was always the picture-taker in the family. What kind of camera do you have?"

"It's a Kodak 8 millimeter movie camera. Would you two just walk around in the yard and act natural. Please?"

I'm gonna be in the movies! I thought. *Wow!*

"Thank you nice folks. I'll come back with my projector and show y'all your movie."

About a month later she did just that.

It came to my attention that one of the local furniture stores was needing a new sign painted. I stopped by and offered to do the job at a reasonable cost, and to my surprise, they hired me. As poor quality as it turned out, that old sign stayed up on the side of that store for many years to come.

My senior year seemed to be the defining time for the rest of my life: the gauge by which I would judge my future and life in general.

After my graduation, and my required signing up for the military draft, my mother and I would move on to Atlanta while Daddy stayed and tied up the open strands of business. He had sold off two slices of the place earlier, one to a local man, adjoining the Jones place on the east, and the other piece on the west next to the Bingham farm to a man from Florida. This wonderful gentleman took such an interest in my artistic talent as to send a letter to his son in Buffalo, New York who worked with a newspaper in advertising. But I really wasn't interested in going north.

In Atlanta I would begin an ambitious new life, away from the little cabin on Blaine Branch. There I would face the realities of life — far beyond the thistle patch.

Rowe, Mike and his son, Wayne, 1971
Beside the cabin of our youth

Epilogue

It was May of 2010. I had been to a Vinson family reunion the day before at the fellowship hall of the new church building which had superceeded the little chapel in which I had fallen and scarred my chin as a child. All five of my remaining uncles were in attendance, and they had come from Ohio, Tennessee and Georgia. I was alone on this particular trip because my wife, Rhonda, was taking care of our granddaughter and couldn't get away.

I had been to the beautiful new library in Franklin and taken a couple of my books to donate, then had done research for this book before stopping by a bank to visit one of my old classmates and pick up information from her.

Before leaving the area I drove out again to the old home palce and knocked on the door of the Ledford house.

I sadly found out that Bud had passed away, and his son, Mike, was now living there. I had a nice visit and caught up on the community news. The most intriguing piece of information that he told me was the fact that the old house which had been moved to Florida had later been purchased by a friend of the original buyer and brought back to North Carolina! According to what Mike Ledford had been told, it was now at Tusquittee, a community in neighboring Clay County near the northern edge of Lake Chatuge.

Somehow, that place will always seem like home. Perhaps some day I will be able to see the old cabin again.

As a young man I had worked days while attending night classes at two stretches in both Georgia and Tennessee in order to earn, first an Associate in Sacred Literature, then a Bachelor in Religious Education. I also took special classes in both art and creative writing. Because of my college enrollment I was granted deferment from the draft and never served in the military. I have often wondered if I had missed a great honor.

I have been richly blessed in spite of many stumbles along life's path. I spent a long and rewarding career in the insurance business as an agent and manager.

I have been priviliged to speak and/or teach in nine Christian denominations and a great many inde-pendent churches.

I have been able to travel around our awesome world, visiting most of these beautiful United States and ten other nations. It has been my distinct honor to have met a good number of the spiritual, political, musical and academic giants of the last half-century, not only Americans, but British and Canadian as well. I count among my friends several brilliant authors, executives and dignitaries. But my old friends and family will never loose their special place in my heart. I have four children, one step-daughter, and fourteen beautiful grandchildren. My first great-grandchild is on the way at this writing. A girl who is to be named Emma Lynn St. Clair.

Creating poetry, articles and books took preeminence over art, and it is something which has given me a great deal of satisfaction and fulfillment.

My three close "bro-cuzes" have also been blessed with fulfulling careers. Lonnie served in the military in Germany, then returned to Georgia to become a leading autobody specialist. Later he also became a top chicken grower for a major producer. Mike went to California to obtain a college degree and ended up back South, owning his own construction business. Gary chose Alaska as a young Army man, working in the rocket program. His adolescent fantacies must have been fulfilled. After returning home, he began to develop and install gorgeous spiral staircases around the state of Georgia. In all of this he still enjoyed his music. Five years ago I was left with a deep emptiness when I learned of his premature passing.

All of us have had good marriages to women who care for us deeply and have been blessed with wonderful children and grandchildren.

It has been forty-six years since that precious era of my life ended. But in my heart I will always return.

The old house as I last saw it

Bibliography

1- Family Genealogy Records, Death Certificates, etc.

2- Henry Buchanan "buchanan" RootsWeb WorldConnect Project hbuchanan@iname.com

3- Sharon Cassidy "Joel Bingham" RootsWeb WorldConnect Project rcass@redrivernet.com

4- Sharon Meehan "Anderson-Beaumont-Spainhour" RootsWeb WorldConnect Project rmeehan@cc.rr.com many sources

5- Franklin High School Class of 1964 Reunion Committee List of Class Deaths 5-2010 - Jane Knight Carnes

6- Heritage of Macon County North Carolina (Vol. 1) 1987 Macon Genealogical Society – page 462

7-Wikipedia article "Great Locomotive Chase" http://en.wikipedia.org/wiki/Great_Locomotive_Chase

8- Elvis Presley's Military Career http://www.history.army.mil/faq/elvis.htm

9- FindaDeath Internet article on Buddy Holly
http://www.findadeath.com/Deceased/h/Buddy%20
Holly/buddy_holly.htm

10- Wikipedia article on John F. Kennedy
Assasination
http://en.wikipedia.org/wiki/John_F._Kennedy_assa
ssination